Gottfried Benn's Static Poetry

UNC | COLLEGE OF ARTS AND SCIENCES
Germanic and Slavic Languages and Literatures

From 1949 to 2004, UNC Press and the UNC Department of Germanic & Slavic Languages and Literatures published the UNC Studies in the Germanic Languages and Literatures series. Monographs, anthologies, and critical editions in the series covered an array of topics including medieval and modern literature, theater, linguistics, philology, onomastics, and the history of ideas. Through the generous support of the National Endowment for the Humanities and the Andrew W. Mellon Foundation, books in the series have been reissued in new paperback and open access digital editions. For a complete list of books visit www.uncpress.org.

Gottfried Benn's Static Poetry
Aesthetic and Intellectual-Historical Interpretations

MARK WILLIAM ROCHE

UNC Studies in the Germanic Languages and Literatures
Number 112

Copyright © 1991

This work is licensed under a Creative Commons CC BY-NC-ND license. To view a copy of the license, visit http://creativecommons.org/licenses.

Suggested citation: Roche, Mark William. *Gottfried Benn's Static Poetry: Aesthetic and Intellectual-Historical Interpretations.* Chapel Hill: University of North Carolina Press, 1991. DOI: https://doi.org/10.5149/9781469656793_Roche

Library of Congress Cataloging-in-Publication Data
Names: Roche, Mark William.
Title: Gottfried Benn's static poetry : Aesthetic and intellectual-historical interpretations / by Mark William Roche.
Other titles: University of North Carolina Studies in the Germanic Languages and Literatures ; no. 112.
Description: Chapel Hill : University of North Carolina Press, [1991] Series: University of North Carolina Studies in the Germanic Languages and Literatures. | Includes bibliographical references and index.
Identifiers: LCCN 90040007 | ISBN 978-1-4696-5678-6 (pbk: alk. paper) | ISBN 978-1-4696-5679-3 (ebook)
Subjects: Benn, Gottfried, 1886-1956 — Criticism and interpretation.
Classification: LCC PT2603.E46 Z775 1991 | DCC 831/ .912

"Trunkene Flut" and "Reisen" are reprinted from: Gottfried Benn. *Sämtliche Gedichte*. Klett-Cotta, Stuttgart 1998. They are printed here with permission of Klett-Cotta.

"Wer allein ist—" and "Statische Gedichte" are reprinted from: Gottfried Benn, *Statische Gedichte* © 1948, 2006 by Arche Literatur Verlag AG, Zürich-Hamburg.

For Barbara

Contents

Acknowledgments	xi
1. Introduction	1
2. "Trunkene Flut"	5
3. "Wer allein ist—"	15
4. "Statische Gedichte"	23
5. "Reisen"	30
6. *Statik* and Inner Emigration	39
7. National Socialism and Transcendental Norms	56
8. Critique	65
9. Theoretical Postscript	75
10. Summary	80
Notes	83
Works Cited	107
Index	119

Acknowledgments

The initial inspiration for this volume came from conversations with Wilfried Barner when I was researching the concept of *Ruhe*, or stillness, in eighteenth- and nineteenth-century German literature.

Hugo Bekker and Egon Schwarz offered suggestions and constructive criticism, as did two anonymous readers. I am equally grateful to Paul T. Roberge and Julia A. McVaugh for their careful and conscientious editorial assistance.

I would also like to thank Gisela Vitt, Chair of the Department of German of Ohio State University, and G. Micheal Riley, Dean of the College of Humanities of Ohio State University, for their generous support of research.

In addition, I am indebted to the College of Humanities and the Office of Research and Graduate Studies of Ohio State University for assistance with the publication of this book.

Finally, I acknowledge permission to quote in their entirety four of Benn's poems: "Trunkene Flut," "Wer allein ist—," "Statische Gedichte," and "Reisen."

Gottfried Benn's Static Poetry

1. Introduction

Gottfried Benn's importance as a poet is to be measured not only by his provocative *Morgue und andere Gedichte* of 1912: bitter revelations, in part with a matter-of-fact scientific tone, of bodily decay, the smell of cancer wards and corpses, the misery of urban existence. Nor can his importance be restricted to his later accounts of the dissolution of the self in the light of modern civilization—as, for example, in his well-known "Verlorenes Ich" of 1943. Rather, Benn is to be equally recognized for his embrace of form, measure, and balance. He is, with Rilke,[1] the twentieth-century poet of stillness.

In a work generally recognized as the best introduction to hermetic modernism, *Die Struktur der modernen Lyrik*, Hugo Friedrich stresses the dual incomprehensibility and fascination of modern poetry. According to Friedrich, modern poetry is characterized by predominantly negative categories: fragmentation, decay, nonassimilability, brutal abruptness, strident imagery, dislocation. The early Benn made a name for himself in part by extending this modern tradition into uncharted territory. His early poetry—"Mann und Frau gehn durch die Krebsbaracke," for example—shocked even those accustomed to the negativity, dissonance, and harshness of the modern lyric. Moreover, significant features of Benn's poetry throughout his career are captured by elements that Friedrich broadly sketches in Baudelaire, Rimbaud, Mallarmé, and their twentieth-century European inheritors: the proud isolation of the poet combined with a depersonalized rhetoric; the hermetic elements of obscure, if not incomprehensible, poetry; the hegemony of form over content and of suggestivity over understanding; the poet as representative sufferer; the interlacing of diverse fields of language; and finally, an undefinable and seemingly empty transcendence that nonetheless serves as a goal. In focusing on Benn's static poetry I would like to stress certain moments, which become more pronounced in later years, in which he deviates from some of the central tenets of the modern lyric. His static poetry is not one of agitation as much as it is one of calm, not one of dissonance as much as it is one of balance, not a break from as much as it is a recollection of premodern traditions, techniques, and definitions of beauty. This poetry is of course not without its mark of modernity, but it is—true to its own theme—more than merely modern.

Benn titled one of his poems and a collection of his poetry "Statische

Gedichte."[2] Many poems outside this cluster of works can also be called *statisch*, in their attempts to embody stillness or stasis.[3] As we will see in the analyses that follow, *Statik*—literally "statics," the branch of mechanics that deals with bodies at rest or forces in equilibrium—is a complex concept. Though the adjective *statisch* gives Benn's poems a technical coloring, the use of this word in conjunction with poetry also takes away from its scientific connotations:[4] *statisch* becomes a metaphor for poetic equilibrium and balance, indeed for motionlessness and permanence as such. Benn's multifaceted use of the term *Statik* also involves a critique of history and, in particular, of national socialism.[5] For him, *Statik* implies an affirmation of stillness in areas as diverse as aesthetics, politics, epistemology, ethics, and metaphysics. In his letter to Peter Schifferli of 23 November 1947 Benn writes: "Statisch ist ein Begriff, der nicht nur meiner inneren ästhetischen und moralischen Lage, sondern auch der formalen Methode der Gedichte entspricht und in die Richtung des durch Konstruktion beherrschten, in sich ruhenden Materials, besser noch: in die Richtung des Anti-Dynamischen verweisen soll . . . Statik also heißt Rückzug auf Maß und Form, es heißt natürlich auch ein gewisser Zweifel an Entwicklung und es heißt auch Resignation, es ist antifaustisch" (DD, 92–93).

Recognizing the overlapping dimensions of *Statik* as well as the value of close readings of individual poems, I do not present a schematic study of the different spheres in which the concept plays a role;[6] rather, I attempt to illuminate the concept's diverse meanings by presenting detailed analyses of four works: "Trunkene Flut" (1927), "Wer allein ist—" (1936), "Statische Gedichte" (1944), and "Reisen" (1950).[7] With these four poems, formally diverse yet similar in the richness of their cryptic allusions, I hope to show a progression from a more dynamic and archaic stillness to a more subdued and cerebral repose. "Trunkene Flut," written well before Benn articulated his concept of *Statik*, is on the surface a dynamic work, full of allusions to motion, struggle, and transformation; nonetheless, I suggest that the poem contains hidden seeds of Benn's later elevation of stillness. "Wer allein ist—" is Benn's starkest affirmation of aesthetic stillness. "Statische Gedichte," another of his best-known works, extends the concept of stillness into the spheres of psychology, ethics, and politics. Finally, "Reisen," written after Benn had seemingly moved beyond the concept of *Statik*, nonetheless reasserts, in its own unique way, some of the principal tenets of stasis—above all, indifference toward the external world. Other poems also support this thesis of a development, but the close analysis of individual works is of more interest to me and, I imagine, of more help to the reader than lengthy sets of lists and quotations.[8] The individual artworks are more at the center of this study than is the linear development of Benn's poetry, though reflection on the latter is made possible as an outgrowth of the former.

The poems illustrate the wide-ranging spheres in which stillness plays a role, and they contain interesting allusions to the tradition of thought on stillness. Benn's knowledge of intellectual history was extensive and precise. He studied theology and classical philology; his letters contain numerous philosophical references; and his poems and essays allude to Greek mythology, Roman history, and German literature. The poems to be analyzed here contain veiled allusions—all but a few previously overlooked—to a tradition of stillness informed by, among others, Parmenides, Aristotle, Epicurus, Seneca, Eckhart, Cusanus, Goethe, Nietzsche, and Rilke.

Stillness, or *Ruhe*, has long been a privileged concept in German letters.[9] In the mystic-pietistic tradition it was elevated for its religious import: stillness was considered not only a characteristic of divinity but also a necessary precondition of human oneness with God. Secularizing this tradition and drawing on the writings of the Stoics and Spinoza, classical authors such as Goethe, Schiller, and Hölderlin associated *Ruhe* with peace of mind. When we achieve repose not only are we at one with ourselves, we have the capacity to act in harmony with the world. In the late eighteenth century *Ruhe* also became a privileged aesthetic category. Winckelmann, who considered sculpture the highest of aesthetic forms, argued that stillness is a facet of all great art. Many authors followed him, elevating stillness as a moment of not only the artwork but its production and reception as well. There is still another sphere in which *Ruhe* has significance: politics. The association of *Ruhe* with order and the status quo has been prevalent throughout German history. In the nineteenth century this association helped undermine the concept's traditionally positive associations. Georg Büchner, Heinrich Heine, and others attacked the elevation of *Ruhe* as conservative and reactionary. It is against this complex prehistory of stillness that Benn's concept of *Statik* merits attention. Benn not only alludes to the religious, psychological, and aesthetic dimensions of stillness, he gives *Statik* a political meaning that adds complexity to the seemingly simple conservative versus liberal assessment of *Ruhe*.

With few exceptions, Benn has been approached from the perspective of immanent interpretation or new criticism or, conversely, from the standpoint of sociological and political criticism.[10] His poetry, both dense and hermetic, does indeed require word-for-word analysis, but it is only by understanding the intellectual-historical context of the poems—the numerous and veiled allusions—that one can fully comprehend their meaning and significance. The "intellectual-historical" thrust of this project has three partially overlapping facets: the attempt to situate Benn's embrace of stasis within the history of the idea of stillness, the endeavor to view stasis as a form of inner emigration, and the attempt to decipher a multiplicity of obscure allusions.

The unraveling of difficult allusions helps us to understand not only Benn's poems and his situation, first within the tradition, and second vis-à-vis his own age, but also the inadequacies in his well-intentioned critique of the national socialist movement. After analyzing the poems as formal constructs, I evaluate their statements. I call my readings "aesthetic" and mean thereby an analysis of rhetorical language and literary structures, followed by an immanent critique of the texts' philosophical statements—that is, a critique that weighs the internal, logical consistency of the works' presuppositions and claims. The term "aesthetic" is appropriate for such a practice insofar as one views art, with Hegel, as a sensuous, if complex and intuitive, representation of ideas, whose validity presupposes logical coherence.[11]

2. "Trunkene Flut"

      Trunkene Flut

Trunkene Flut,
trance- und traumgefleckt,
o Absolut,
das meine Stirne deckt,
um das ich ringe,
aus dem der Preis
der tiefen Dinge,
die die Seele weiß.

In Sternenfieber,
das nie ein Auge maß,
Nächte, Lieber,
daß man des Tods vergaß,
im Zeiten-Einen,
im Schöpfungsschrei
kommt das Vereinen,
nimmt hin—vorbei.

Dann du alleine
nach großer Nacht,
Korn und Weine
dargebracht,
die Wälder nieder,
die Hörner leer,
zu Gräbern wieder
steigt Demeter,

dir noch im Rücken,
im Knochenbau,
dann ein Entzücken,
ein Golf aus Blau,
von Tränen alt,
aus Not und Gebrest
eine Schöpfergestalt,
die uns leben läßt,

6 *"Trunkene Flut"*

    die viel gelitten,
    die vieles sah,
    immer in Schritten
    dem Ufer nah
    der trunkenen Flut,
    die die Seele deckt
    groß wie der Fingerhut
    sommers die Berge fleckt.

(GW, 3:60–61)

"Trunkene Flut," first published in 1927 and then rereleased in 1949 as the title poem of a collection, presents a challenge to any critic wanting to argue for the priority of stillness in Benn's poetry. Already in the poem's title we find a pair of Dionysian images, and the first two stanzas introduce still more. Dionysus is the god of intoxication and flux, the counterpart of Apollinian stability. At the very opening the poet invokes him with an emotional *exclamatio*: "o Absolut, / das meine Stirne deckt." This initial address suggests, first, that the poet rivets all his attention on the absolute Dionysian principle; second, that the Dionysian moment obliterates the poet's capacity for reflection—in Benn's work, *Stirne* approximates the meaning of *Gehirn*;[1] and third, that the absolute principle erases the individuality of the poet— much as the Dionysian element dissolves Apollinian individuality. The word *Sternenfieber* suggests that Dionysian frenzy or fever has invaded even the Apollinian realm of light and health. Dionysus, whose mysteries are performed chiefly in the dark, represents night ("Nächte") as opposed to Apollinian clarity and measure ("das nie ein Auge maß"). He negates individuality and temporality ("daß man des Tods vergaß"). Further, he is the god of violent, eruptive sexuality and creation ("Schöpfungsschrei") as well as of mystical unity and nondifferentiation ("im Zeiten-Einen . . . das Vereinen"). It is in this Dionysian frenzy that the poet experiences both mystical union and poetic inspiration.

The Dionysian unity passes after stanza 2. Both the poetic inspiration and the sexual act ("das Vereinen") are "vorbei": "Dann du alleine / nach großer Nacht." The imagery of sexuality remains, however, in such phrases as "die Hörner leer" or "dir noch im Rücken." The sexual motifs represent the primitive, prerational, and inspirational origins of the poetic process. Such imagery also helps Benn avoid any pretense of sentimentality. The mythological and cosmic references, meanwhile, allow the poet to transcend his own subjectivity.[2] The poem is more than its author. F. W. Wodtke sees in the image of the trance-filled *Flut* an allusion to the Jungian collective unconscious (*SP*, 146). For Jung, the most prevalant symbol of the unconscious is water. The Dionysian water or "trunkene Flut" opens the poet's eyes to the riches of the unconscious, and thus also of past times, from which the poet draws both the inspiration and the content of his poem.

The third stanza parallels the sexual act and Dionysian unity with the harvest: bread-corn, the gift of Demeter, and wine, the present of Dionysus, have been offered. The mystical and religious motifs that surfaced in the images of love and union recur here with the idea that the poet's creation is also a kind of sacrificial offering. In immersing himself in Dionysian intoxication, the poet sacrifices his own individuality. He becomes the mouthpiece of an earlier people: "Wir tragen die frühen Völker in unserer Seele und wenn die späte Ratio sich lockert, in Traum und Rausch, steigen sie empor mit ihren Riten, ihrer prälogischen Geistesart und vergeben eine Stunde der mystischen Partizipation . . . das Alte, das Unbewußte . . . erscheint in der magischen Ichumwandlung und Identifizierung, im frühen Erlebnis des Überall und des Ewigseins" (*GW*, 1:99).[3]

With the harvest past, the seasons again begin to revolve. Demeter laments Hades' abduction of her daughter Persephone or Core. During this time the earth is barren. Thereafter Demeter, with her daughter, appears to ascend upward toward the graves of humanity and thus out of the depths of the netherworld.[4] Demeter ascends, however, as a skeletal figure. The idea seems to be that the continual material harvest is only the frame for the greater development of consciousness and history. Or, since the syntax is ambiguous, the skeleton may refer to the poetic "you," who finds little left of self or of inspiration after the Dionysian moment is past. The poet shares with Demeter an interest in revival. While "die Hörner leer" refers to the end of the harvest and of sexual bounty, it also signifies the end of Dionysian unity. As Benn notes in his description of the Dionysian dance, the maenads often wore horns on their heads.[5] Further, the Dionysian moment of sexual unity is related to the function of Demeter. Demeter laments not only as the mother of Persephone but as the goddess of fertility.

After his allusion to seasonal cycles and the end of Dionysian ecstasy, the poet moves on to an account of human history. He begins with the Mediterranean ("ein Golf aus Blau"), the long-lamented origin of Western history ("von Tränen alt"). In Benn's private imagery blue also symbolizes the origins of psychic development—that is, the unconscious.[6] The poet then introduces "eine Schöpfergestalt, / die uns leben läßt." This may refer to Prometheus, who championed and, in some versions, created humankind, but for reasons that will follow, the figure is more likely Christ, a creator who died ("aus Not und Gebrest") so that we could continue to live.[7] Christ is followed by the great sufferer and wanderer Odysseus ("die viel gelitten, / die vieles sah"), who with much effort finally returned to the shore of Ithaca ("immer in Schritten / dem Ufer nah"). Anachronistically, Odysseus follows Christ. The blending of seemingly diverse and different historical epochs is prefigured in the earlier Dionysian formulation "Zeiten-Einen." We see here a montage technique characteristic for Benn during this period, the simultaneity of diverse historical epochs. Universal history is presented in an almost atemporal manner. The chronological becomes simultaneous. Though Benn frequently expresses his disdain for history, and does so with increasing emphasis, intellectual history remains for him the least directionless of the various forms of history, and his paradoxical, if not contradictory, notion of atemporal history is central to his understanding of poetic origination. To make things more complicated we can add that "die viel gelitten, / die vieles sah" need not refer only to Odysseus: it is equally Christ, who traveled about, teaching the masses, and suffered from his crucifixion.[8] The poet, as we will see, not only lets these figures melt into one, he himself identifies with the heroes and gods he invokes.

Parallel to Demeter, the poet brings us the fruits of intellectual labor. Much like Prometheus or Christ, he is a creator (consider the *Schöpfungsschrei*). The poet's unity with these mythological and historical figures extends still further. Demeter, Prometheus, Christ, Odysseus, and the poet share moments of suffering: Demeter mourns the loss of Persephone; Prometheus was doomed to perpetual agony for his defiance of Zeus;[9] Christ was crucified; Odysseus suffers in his attempts to return to Ithaca, and when in book 12 he has his men tie him to the mast as they pass the Sirens he, too, appears as a crucified figure; the poet, meanwhile, experiences to an extreme degree the suffering of modern humanity.[10] Because all but Prometheus share a relationship to the revival of the dead, "eine Schöpfergestalt, / die uns leben lässt" most likely refers to Christ. Dionysus eliminates death through nondifferentiation; in addition, he is traditionally associated with immortality and the cult of the dead.[11] Demeter, with whom the poet most readily identifies here, arranges Persephone's return from Hades by refusing otherwise to restore the earth to fruitfulness, and in one version of the myth she herself descends into Hades to retrieve her daughter. The other figures are equally associated with renewal: Christ preaches the afterlife, "die Auferstehung der Toten,"[12] and in book 11 Odysseus calls from the netherworld the souls of many great heroes.[13] The poet, too, awakens images of the past from out of his own soul; his mission is to make the Dionysian once again fruitful and to overcome temporality by forming a product of eternity. Not only are Dionysus and Odysseus mirror images of the poet, they represent the very target of the poet's revival. Odysseus is directly linked to Dionysus and thus to poetic celebration; he returns to Ithaca in a state of sleep or unconsciousness and is therefore, for Benn, immersed in the Dionysian (*GW*, 3:109). In his early writings Benn specifically equates Dionysus and Odysseus through this moment of unconsciousness (*GW*, 2:303).

The title of Benn's poem alludes to the first stanza of Annette von Droste-Hülshoff's "Im Grase."[14] Her poem begins:

Süße Ruh', süßer Taumel im Gras,
Von des Krautes Arom umhaucht,
Tiefe Flut, tief, tieftrunkne Flut,
Wenn die Wolk' am Azure verraucht,
Wenn aufs müde, schwimmende Haupt
Süßes Lachen gaukelt herab,
Liebe Stimme säuselt, und träuft
Wie die Lindenblüt' auf ein Grab.
 (102)

Like Droste, Benn stresses the unity of *Ruhe* and *Flut*. He also portrays in the Dionysian moment the awakening of the dead. Not only the content of Droste's poem but also her style is invoked in Benn's work; it was Droste who introduced the ellipsis as a stylistic principle to Germany. The motion downward to a grave in Droste's poem contrasts, however, with Demeter's ascension in Benn's poem: because Demeter comes from the depths of the netherworld she ascends to the graves. One can say that Benn's poem is consciously concerned with a lower, more subconscious level of self and world. There is, however, another interpretation of Demeter's movement toward the graves, and it brings us to Benn's fascination with Goethe's mythology of *die Mütter* in *Faust*:[15] they, like Demeter, are of course mothers; again like Demeter, they concern themselves with the preservation of those in the underworld; and, most importantly, as Mephistopheles says, their realm knows neither up nor down: "Versinke denn! Ich könnt' auch sagen: steige!" (6275). We recognize in Demeter's journey Benn's disregard for a realistic perception of space. The verb *steigen* need not mean "to climb" or "to ascend": it can also signify *hinuntergehen*, so that one could easily say, "daß man in den Hades steigt." As suggested above, Demeter may be returning from Hades and ascending to the graves on the earth's surface, hence making possible the bounteous words "dann ein Entzücken," but it is also conceivable that she is descending to the depths of the netherworld, symbolized by the graves, and thus only embarking on her journey. The pertinent lines, after all, immediately follow a description of depletion ("die Hörner leer"). The passage is ambiguous and serves, along with Benn's use of the word *wieder*, to underscore the cyclical structure of the Demeter myth. Just as time folds in on itself, so too are the distinctions of space (and of language) dissolved in Benn's world of Dionysian unity and poetic creation. We are far removed from the clarity and spatial realism of Droste.

In the final stanza the poet, identifying with Odysseus, slowly moves to the banks of the Dionysian *trunkene Flut*. The poet is completing his work, "Trunkene Flut," which covers the soul the way *Fingerhut* spots the mountains in the summer. The imagery of the *Fingerhut*—if taken in its everyday meaning—is symbolic of sexual union, the Dionysian union of Apollinian individuals. But *Fingerhut* does not only mean "thimble": it is a plant—a poisonous (and thus Dionysian) plant, but also a plant used for cures (and in this sense Apollinian). The imagery has yet another dimension. The creation of the poem, the Apollinian moment, releases the poet from his own subjectivity; what is important is not his personal suffering but his artistic creation. Here the Apollinian moment cures the poetic self even as the poet sacrifices himself.[16] The *trunkene Flut* qua poem is paralleled with the *Fingerhut* and exhibits poetry's therapeutic function. But the parallel extends to the Dionysian moment as well. In the myths of Dionysian cults the votary escapes his tortured individuality and overcomes his suffering through moments of intoxication and celebration. In Benn's "Heinrich Mann. Ein Untergang" the narrator's suffering dissolves into a "Wirbel von Glück" as soon as he celebrates a Bacchanalian festival (GW, 2:12). The *trunkene Flut* qua Dionysian unity and transsubjective surge of images likewise frees the poet from his individual pains.

The proximity of Dionysian and Apollinian in the imagery of the foxglove mirrors their conflation in the entire poem. Dionysian dynamism is present throughout. The overriding image is of process. Each short line, hardly independent, runs on into the next. The half-sentences frequently end with, and thus highlight, the predicates. Enjambments surface on almost every line, and the poem leads into the final stanza with a strophe enjambment. But the process turns back on itself. The poem is circular as well as linear; its motion is self-contained. The rhyming scheme adds to the circular structure both on the level of finite repetition and on the wider level of the poem itself: the final stanza's *c* and *d* rhymes are the first stanza's *a* and *b* rhymes, and the words at the end of three of the poem's final four lines ("Flut," "deckt," and "fleckt") recall the occurrence of these same words in the opening lines.[17] Rhythmically and linguistically, the poem's ending binds itself to its beginning. The apparent stress on predicates is weakened by the fact that there are only three verbs in main clauses throughout the entire poem ("kommt," "nimmt hin," and "steigt").[18] The motion is not finite. The geographical up and down is also circular—first, in the movement of Demeter and the other figures, and second, in the movement from the flatlands to the hills and back again. The motion of water implicitly echoes this circularity both in the finite wave and in the general ecocycle. The emphasis on seasons (the harvest, Demeter, "sommers") adds to the theme of circularity, as does the merging of figures from diverse periods. Circles are of course traditional symbols of stillness.[19] The repetition evoked by circularity, whether historical or natural, conveys stillness. The rhymes, as suggested, convey circularity and stillness as well. In this way the form of the poem becomes its content. By transforming the linear movement of the poem into a circle, Benn's artwork becomes almost spatial: it borders on sculpture.[20] The circularity of the work makes it a closed and finite form, an Apollinian work, but here, too, the Dionysian shows its force. Circularity is also a Dionysian symbol; the circular structure of the ring dance is central to the cult of Dionysus. Borrowing from the language of Howard Nemerov, an American poet steeped in the German tradition, one can say that in its stillness the poem still moves.[21]

The early lines "o Absolut, / das meine Stirne deckt, / um das ich ringe" may be said to reinforce the circular imagery by way of the nonliteral reference to a ring. However, the verb *ringen* might also be read as invoking openness: it implies struggle and a continuing effort to grasp the absolute. The tension between figurative and literal meanings seems to undermine closure and may imply that the struggle of *ringen* has as much to do with representation and the trickiness of language as with the difficulties involved in creating or experiencing a moment of mystical truth. The juxtaposition of the nonliteral and literal evokes an uncertainty, by which the absolute may be grasped, may be removed, or, if one thinks the two together and views them in the context of the whole poem, may be grasped in the very moment of dynamic struggle. The fact that the poem portrays both struggle and closure reinforces such a synthetic reading, as does the apposition in lines one and three, which suggests an identity of the absolute with the *trunkene Flut*—that is, with the poem itself. Finally, the literal moment, the struggle, comes early in the poem, while the conclusion of the poem returns us via its global rhyming scheme to circularity, thus suggesting that the poem itself may lead to an overcoming of struggle. The nonliteral, the poetic, prevails, and with it the concept of mediation.

A similar ambiguity arises with the third line from the end, "die die Seele deckt," where the relative pronoun refers to "die trunkene Flut" and thus, metonymically, to the poem as a whole. The poem's covering the soul may imply fulfillment, a suggestion that the poet's message is comfortably and fully enclosed within the poem. However, the verb *decken* is ambiguous: it also means to cover, to hide, to eliminate from view, so that the soul's desire to express itself in the poem may be not fulfilled, but thwarted. Does *decken* imply in this instance fulfillment and union, or erasure and displacement? Is the soul contained within, or concealed from view? One solution to the quandary would be to read *Seele* not just as the poet's message but also as the poet's self; in this way the seemingly opposed meanings of fulfillment and concealment would be united. We recall the earlier tragic structure, whereby the poet sacrifices himself for the completion of the poetic work.

In yet another reading of this line, the relative pronoun is the object, rather than the subject, of the clause: here "die Seele," viewed as subject, covers "die trunkene Flut." This reading must also draw on the ambiguity of the verb *decken*: either the soul—perhaps that of the reader as well as that of the poet—grasps the essence of the poem, or the poem eludes the soul. The ambiguity in vocabulary and syntax reinforces the complexity of the line's message. The extended metaphor ("wie der Fingerhut / sommers die Berge fleckt") may help clarify the interpretation: the foxglove speckles the mountains as the poem covers the soul—or, in the variant reading, the soul covers the poem. The foxglove *speckles* the mountains in such a way as to suggest a partial covering, but a covering nonetheless. The beauty of the poem is conveyed, though the poem is not exhausted by any one soul. Because the relative pronoun can refer to either noun, the poem and the soul are elliptically identified: there is thus further evidence for the suggestion that the poetic self finds its identity in the poem. In addition, the union reaffirms poetic mediation. The poem and the soul, which are separated by the negative connotations of *decken*, overlap in the verb's positive connotations and in the common pronoun.

The poem conveys images of mediation and rupture, closure and openness, fulfillment and concealment, stability and flux. The prominent reference to blue is also ambiguous. The poem tells of history from antiquity, symbolized in the Mediterranean blue ("das Südwort schlechthin" [*GW*, 1:512]), through Christ, and toward the present.[22] The mountains speckled with foxglove are, one presumes, those of Italy and Germany, as in Herder's and Hölderlin's influential schemes: first, because the poem treats the development of history geographically, from the level and horizontal dimensions Benn associated with the South[23] to the mountains of the North, and temporally from Mediterranean antiquity to the present; second, because the foxglove is indigenous to the mountains of Central Europe. The Mediterranean blue, however, is not just the source of modern history, it is the stillness of the sea. An important Greek word for *Ruhe* is γαλήνη (*Meeresstille*). Such idyllic stillness is conveyed in the poem as ideal origin and goal; it is not only the beginning, but the end of history. Here one thinks of Schiller's and Hölderlin's prominent associations of stillness and the color blue with the heavens and thus with the ideal.[24] It is this harmony to which humankind wants to return, "zurück, wo still die Wasser stehn" (*GW*, 3:224). The longing for the qualities of the Mediterranean is of course a prominent idea in Benn, expressed very early in poems such as "Gesänge" (*GW*, 3:25–26) and "D-Zug" (*GW*, 3:27–28), or in the contemporary "Orphische Zellen" (*GW*, 3:76–77).

Finally, "Trunkene Flut" is an individual work of art. The Dionysian, which even at the poem's origin was "traumgefleckt,"[25] has been superseded by the Apollinian. What Benn has thematized—the process of creation and recognition, the union of the Dionysian and the Apollinian—he has also formed. The poem is not just Dionysian *Rausch* but "Formrausch" (*GW*, 2:133). In his essay on "Expressionismus" Benn phrases the process thus: "Dionysos endet und ruht zu Füßen des klaren delphischen Gottes" (*GW*, 1:252). The Dionysian represents the transsubjective and undifferentiated origin that passes over into the constructed Apollinian product. The individual recognizes and forms the depths ("die Seele weiß"). Like Hölderlin, Benn's poet makes the Dionysian visible. Creation, even though it is not primarily cerebral, is nonetheless a *formation* out of chaos. The poem need not be line-for-line static, but as an entirety it is closed within itself.[26]

"Trunkene Flut" was written before Benn articulated his theory of static poetry, but with this reading we can understand why, after he was immersed in the principle of aesthetic stillness, he could reach back and privilege this poem, making it the title of a new cluster of works. In his later poetry, however, the unity of the expressionist *Schrei* or Dionysian *Flut* with Apollinian form and stasis will clearly shift in favor of stillness.[27]

3. "Wer allein ist—"

Wer allein ist—

Wer allein ist, ist auch im Geheimnis,
immer steht er in der Bilder Flut,
ihrer Zeugung, ihrer Keimnis,
selbst die Schatten tragen ihre Glut.

Trächtig ist er jeder Schichtung
denkerisch erfüllt und aufgespart,
mächtig ist er der Vernichtung
allem Menschlichen, das nährt und paart.

Ohne Rührung sieht er, wie die Erde
eine andere ward, als ihm begann,
nicht mehr Stirb und nicht mehr Werde:
formstill sieht ihn die Vollendung an.

(GW, 3:135)

"Wer allein ist—" (1936) also celebrates stillness, but in a very different way. It is an apodictic poem, spoken laconically from a perspective of authoritative distance. The poet's distance from the reader as well as his movement beyond his own subjectivity can be seen in his use of the indefinite pronoun ("wer") and the third person singular ("er").[1] The poet does not offer his personal view of the world; he would claim that what he says is a priori true. This moment of abstraction continues to the end of the poem. When in the tradition general aesthetic principles are announced in a poem, they tend to derive from a particular work of art; one thinks, for example, of Mörike's "Auf eine Lampe" (10). Here, in contrast, the poet names no particular work; he speaks of the poem or of art as such. Benn is concerned with the universal. In "Wer allein ist—" the temporal dimension disappears altogether. Correspondingly, the moment of dynamism is underplayed. In an inversion of what we saw in "Trunkene Flut" the poet is removed from the sphere of flux even as the poem asserts that he has control over it (stanza 1). The stress is not on dynamism but on the Apollinian moment of reflection (stanza 2) and the Apollinian product (stanza 3).

Whoever is alone, is immersed in mystery—not only the copula but the common diphthong and the rhetorical figure of chiasmus link the essential words. As in the mystic and idealist traditions, solitude and stillness are prerequisites for mystical union or poetic inspiration. *Geheimnis* suggests hermeticism as well as mysticism. The poem appears to be saying that the experience cannot (or should not) be fully articulated and passed on to another. However, the connection to those traditions that celebrate the ineffable is only apparent. Benn would have us view the poem, in its *Vollendung*, as the formulation of this mystery. Amidst the continuous flow of images and movement of everyday life the poet stands still. The passage of time does not disturb his repose. The images of flux in the first stanza allude to Heraclitus, of whom Benn once wrote in a clear echo, if not plagiarism, of Nietzsche: "die von ihm erblickte Welt zeigte nirgends ein Verharren, eine Unzerstörbarkeit, eine Andeutung von Dauer" (*GW*, 1:386–87).[2] Plato frequently summarizes Heraclitus's philosophy in the epigram πάντα ῥεῖ or "all things flow" (*Cratylus*, 401d and elsewhere), a phrase with which Benn was quite familiar. Drawing on both Heraclitus and Protagoras, Benn writes: "Panta rhei—das ist Natur; der Mensch das Maß aller Dinge, das ist Geist" (*GW*, 4:256). In his famous river fragment Heraclitus states—here in Benn's formulation—"daß alles fließt und daß es dieselben Flüsse nicht mehr sind, auch wenn wir in dieselben Flüsse steigen" (*GW*, 3:594).[3] Though Heraclitus's doctrine of flux seems to apply to all life, the poet is here excluded.[4] Rhyming with *Flut* is *Glut*, Heraclitus's other image for transformation, namely, the restless flame. The flame is so great that it reaches not only what is itself ablaze but even the shadows, one step removed. The passage is quite playful. Shadows are always separate from the light or flame that creates them. Thus an image of all-embracing restlessness is conveyed insofar as flux, symbolized in the flames, reaches even the shadows. Traditionally, however, shadows convey restlessness: they function much like water or flames, and so it is not surprising that they, too, as in Plato's cave allegory (*Republic*, 508–13), represent change and becoming. In Benn's poem this world of change and development is material, primarily biological: "Zeugung . . . Keimnis." The second stanza's references to biology become mundane, even sarcastic: eating and mating. The poet, who appears to be beyond this sphere, focuses in his solitude and stillness on the idea, the essence, *das Geheimnis*. His intellectual creation is of a different, more stable order.

The word *Schichtung* comes from the realm of geology and has the specific meaning of stratification.[5] In Benn's vocabulary, stratified spheres are the accumulated layers of mankind's history over which the poet has an intuitive grasp: "Ihr großer Gedanke [Benn refers to psychology] ist der Schichtungscharakter des Psychischen, das geologische Prinzip. Die Seele ist in Schichten entstanden und gebaut, und, was wir vorhin im Organischen gelegentlich der Bildung des Großhirns entwicklungsanatomisch aus verschollenen Äonen vernahmen, offenbart der Traum, offenbart das Kind, offenbart die Psychose als noch vorhandene seelische Realität" (GW, 1:98–99). No particular history plays a role in Benn's world. History enters his poetry only insofar as its general remains contribute to the poet's formulation of the absolute. *Schichtung* is the presubjective realm that in "Trunkene Flut" was associated with the movement of water; here, even the transsubjective has geological stability. The poet's interests lie not with the surface flow of life, but with its depths; not development, but stasis: "Ach, diese ewige Entwicklung, welch eine kommerzielle Kontinuität! Die Seele hat andere Tendenzen, sie hat eine Schichtungs- und Rückkehrtendenz" (GW, 1:409).

Schichtung nonetheless remains subservient to spirit. History, even in its accumulated layers, is still expressed in the language of nature—that is, with geological metaphors—whereas the poem is represented through privileged allusions to the intellect. For Benn, the poet approximates the role Hegel grants to the philosopher in his *Phänomenologie des Geistes*: the poet inherits and has command over past history, and his task is to articulate this history in its relationship to the absolute and to the present. In fact, the combination of *erfüllt* and *aufgespart* captures two of the three meanings conveyed through the Hegelian *aufheben*: raise or fulfill; save or preserve; and cancel or negate.[6] The only meaning dropped is the third one, which brings forth images of flux and temporality—of this the poet will have nothing. Immersed in thought, he raises the images of human history to a final poetic formulation. With his focus on the mysteries of the absolute, the poet is beyond the destruction that inevitably befalls humans in growth and love. In "Trunkene Flut" poetic creation was associated with sexual union; here the speaker, stressing the unique and cerebral dimensions of creation, distances himself from the all-too-biological analogy. Whereas the individual's material nourishment and reproduction belong in time, the poet's pregnancy of thought supersedes material and temporal spheres. *Denkerisch* is a key word here. The moment of gemination in stanza 1 passes over into a moment of reflection, and the poet contrasts his own intellectual work with the general biological sphere of humanity. Subjective consciousness transcends concrete moments of intersubjective experience.

Rührung was not formulated in its present sense until the eighteenth century. Its original meaning is simply "motion," a denotation that is especially infrequent today, although the German for "At ease!" is still *Rührt euch! Rührung* primarily means "with affect." In its broadest sense the verb *rühren* is related to the Latin *movere* and *commovere* or the English *to move* and *to be moved*. The advocate or politician tries to move the public, change its position, influence its action. The poet, who is "ohne Rührung," not only lacks affect,[7] he has no desire to create an effect.[8] Not an actor in life, he is an observer, a voyeur.

The poet looks on while the earth changes, but the earth's motion does not disturb him. The earth is the sphere of nature and (as it revolves) the sphere of history. The reference to the moving earth might well be read as an allusion to the Kusmitsch episode of Rilke's *Aufzeichnungen des Malte Laurids Brigge*.[9] Rilke's character Nikolaj Kusmitsch, having assumed he will probably live another fifty years, has decided to change his years into days, hours, minutes, even seconds, and has calculated the total. Though he tries to save time by rushing, he notices that at the end of each week there is nothing left of all his saving. As Kusmitsch senses time passing by, he feels the earth moving. He cannot tolerate this movement, so he decides to lie down and keep quiet: "Liegen und ruhig halten, hatte er einmal irgendwo gelesen. Und seither lag Nikolaj Kusmitsch" (161). Though he admires those who can bear "die Bewegung der Erde" (162), Kusmitsch himself wants to be as stable as possible. He finds his solution in the reciting of poetry. Though Rilke ironizes Kusmitsch's thoughts, Benn seriously adopts a similar stance as his own. Benn's poet is oblivious to the movement of the earth, and with poetry he would overcome the flux of change and becoming.

The poet is not immersed, as are nature and history, in the dynamic decay and regeneration, the "Stirb und Werde" of Goethe's "Selige Sehnsucht," a poem that celebrates those who perish in flames.[10] Goethe's "Stirb und Werde" implies integration into a greater life, an organic whole. Benn's poet withdraws from this broader sphere. He does not portray, as in "Trunkene Flut," a montage of historical reality. He does not move into a dynamic world that nonetheless includes a moment of duration; he remains in a realm of stability and stasis. One does not get the sense that the poet laments this loss of regeneration; on the contrary, he is content with absolute stasis. Goethe's *Mütter*, who orchestrate "die ewige Metamorphose des irdischen Daseins, des Entstehens und Wachsens, des Zerstörens und Wiederbildens" (Eckermann, 385), are no longer the heroines of Benn's poetry. Without completely denying a moment of origination to the poem (consider the implications of the word *trächtig*), Benn moves beyond Goethe and the dynamism of his own "Trunkene Flut." In an anti-

Goethean passage of a letter to his friend F. W. Oelze, Benn writes: "Die *Verwandlung* ist das Gesetz des Lebens, die *Erstarrung* d.h. die Formwerdung das Gesetz des Geistes" (emphasis in the original, *Oelze* no. 88 [28 July 1936]). Instead of the content of dynamism, Benn stresses stasis. Instead of the rhythmic form of dynamism, he presents gnomic assertions.

The word *sieht* surfaces twice in the final stanza. The poet not only *sees* the world decay, he *is seen* by perfection. The artwork has liberated itself from the subject. The poem, no longer a part of the poet's subjectivity, has an objective status. The poet looks indifferently at nature and history; he does not concern himself with the problems of the world, or of the individuals in it. The object, meanwhile—the artwork—seems to have more vitality and purpose than the poet. The poem is not only autonomous and active as its own subject, it is more powerful than the subject who created it. The moment is reminiscent of the poet in the age of idealism. Though Theo Meyer cites Novalis (330), the autonomy of the artwork for Novalis has less to do with stable perfection than with the romantic polyvalence of meaning that necessarily transcends the intentions of a work's creator. One would do better to think of Hölderlin—for example, the poet's sacrifice in "An die Deutschen" (2:9–11), or the crisis of "Wie wenn am Feiertage" (2:118–20). The created poem is greater than the poet; and the poet, as in "Trunkene Flut," would gladly sacrifice himself for such perfection.[11] What looks quietly back at the poet is his poem, a creation of eternity; not the motion and strife of the world, but stillness. This stillness is an embodiment of artistic perfection.

One is reminded of a passage in Hegel's *Aesthetics* where the philosopher, arguing for the unity of form and content, suggests that, if the eye is the window of the soul, then the great artwork turns every point of its surface into eyes, "zu einem tausendäugigen Argus, damit die innere Seele und Geistigkeit an allen Punkten gesehen werde" (13:203). The work of art looks out at its viewers as an organic being, revealing its inner essence.[12] The questioning of language and the awareness of ambiguity that we saw (at least momentarily) in "Trunkene Flut" disappear in this confident assertion of artistic realization and autonomy. Time is sublated—not in the Dionysian unconscious, as in "Trunkene Flut," but rather in the artwork itself. The stability of perfected form is the poet's answer to the dissolution and transformation that rule history: "Ströme und Gegenströme, Strebungen und Gegenstrebungen, nichts Sicheres, nichts Festes, wohin er blickt. In der Welt hat jeder und jedes recht, alles fließt, so sinke denn, man kann auch sagen steige . . . alles hin und her, alles ambivalent. Dagegen erhebt sich sein inneres Gesetz. Er hat seinen Zwang sich auszudrücken, Gebilde zu schaffen" (*GW*, 4:436). The poet counters the contemporary breakdown of values and the chaotic senselessness of historical movements with ideal stillness, "Ruhe und Statik" (*GW*, 4:436).

The poem's rhymes suggest stasis as well. The poem does not move on as much as it returns to its earlier stages. The middle stanza, stressing repetition, even adds an initial rhyme: *mächtig* and *trächtig*. The rhymes are helpful for an interpretation of the poem's content and can be evaluated for their semantic similarities and dissimilarities. *Geheimnis* pairs with *Keimnis* but is also its opposite: the first is the sphere of stable poetic being, the second refers to the origins of the images of appearance. *Flut* and *Glut* bring us back to a common unity: they are the water and fire of Heraclitean flux. In the second stanza *Schichtung* and *Vernichtung* are juxtaposed as two forms of history: static culmination or preservation, and the decay that befalls individuals within the process of history. The contrast continues with the rhymes in lines two and four of the second stanza: the poet saves images, intellectually, while those who biologically unite will eventually pass away. The word *paart* thematizes what it does, even as it underscores the differences between poetic and worldly spheres. Since *paart* refers not only to mating but also to the poet's act of rhyming words, the poet is here transformed, perhaps unwittingly, into the context of human temporality. While the poet creates, he represents a principle of stillness (stanzas 1 and 2). After his creation he enters the sphere of human temporality (the transition to the final stanza); the poem alone would seem to stand still. In this last stanza *Erde* and *Werde* are united. The earthly realm is the realm of becoming. Meanwhile, "begann" and "Vollendung an" contrast, the first representing temporality, the second the timelessness of the poem. Origination passes over into perfection. While the *a* rhymes in the *a b a b* stanzas are unaccented, the *b* rhymes—including the final syllables of each stanza, and of course of the poem—are accented; this conveys, linguistically, a certain finality to the work.

Not only its ending but the poem as a whole is *formstill*, static and permanent. The work almost passes over into silence; it does not speak, it sees. Though one may want to read this as a reference to the ineffable, it is more likely an allusion to the poem's wholeness. Seeing, unlike speaking, does not demand a narrative; it is immediately whole. Not only is our experience of the poem one of stillness, the poem itself embodies this quality. Benn counters the organic concept of the never-completed, fragmentary art of the Romantics (the "Nächstens mehr" of *Hyperion*, the "Stern-bald" of Tieck's *Wanderungen*, etc.) with absolute poetry, in which all elements are final.[13] Where the secondary meaning of *Vollendung* is "perfection," its primary denotation is "completion." In looking ahead to the etymological games of "Reisen" we can say that the fragmentary poetry of the Romantics, Faustian poetry if you will, is immersed in the infinite (ἄπειρον), whereas Benn's poetry of self-sufficient form and finality asserts and embraces the concept of a limit (πέρας).[14] As in Plato's *Philebus* (25b–27e), it is the limit that creates measure, balance, beauty. In dismissing from the perfected artwork any element of flux, Benn approximates the stance and rhetoric of Heraclitus's Eleatic counterpart Parmenides, the philosopher of stable being. Indeed, Benn often refers to his art—as he does here only implicitly—as a closed, round, perfect, and resting sphere: "ich kenne nämlich eine Sphäre, die ohne diese Art von Beweglichkeit ist, eine Sphäre, die ruht, die nie aufgehoben werden kann, die abschließt: die ästhetische Sphäre" (*GW*, 4:159). One hears in the background the perfect and self-limiting repose of Parmenides' famous σφαῖρα,[15] though Benn's sphere of stable and perfected being is exclusively the sphere of art.[16]

In German *Klassik*, where the ideal aesthetic form, like Benn's, calls for stillness, *Ruhe* and *Vollendung* are frequently intertwined.[17] Benn draws on this classical ideal of perfect stillness, voiced most famously by Winckelmann (20–21). Not only does he, like Winckelmann, elevate stillness to the forefront of aesthetics; in consequence, he also reestablishes sculpture as an ideal form of art.[18] It would seem unlikely for a twentieth-century poet to view sculpture (or architecture) as an elevated art form when one considers the influence of Hegel's aesthetics, in which Hegel argues that poetry is the superior art form to the extent that its primary content is spirit. But one must remember that for the later Benn, poetry has no content; it is pure form. Moreover, one can view Benn's elevation of sculpture as a critique of postclassical aesthetics, in which sculpture is disparaged for its alleged timelessness and association with historical-political indifference. For Heine, to take one of the earliest and most prominent examples, sculpture lacks temporality; the following passage documents his critique of Goethe's writings as a kind of apathetic sculpture: "Sie [die Goetheschen Meisterwerke] zieren unser teueres Vaterland, wie schöne Statuen einen Garten zieren, aber es sind Statuen. Man kann sich darin verlieben, aber sie sind unfruchtbar" (3:395). Benn, who stands opposed to the liberal inheritors of Heine's position, returns to what he sees as classicism's embrace of timelessness and autonomy in art, and he does so by transforming poetry into a kind of sculpture. Benn, however, modulates the classical concept of aesthetic stillness in three ways: first, he idealizes, not the heroes or gods embodied in sculpture, but beautifully crafted and stable stone as such—a "Marmorstufe," for example (GW, 2:346); second, he replaces dynamic stillness with an increasingly constructed and static stillness; and third, he suggests that the stillness of art is not the sensuous portrayal of the absolute, but the absolute itself.

4. "Statische Gedichte"

> Statische Gedichte
>
> Entwicklungsfremdheit
> ist die Tiefe des Weisen,
> Kinder und Kindeskinder
> beunruhigen ihn nicht,
> dringen nicht in ihn ein.
>
> Richtungen vertreten,
> Handeln,
> Zu- und Abreisen
> ist das Zeichen einer Welt,
> die nicht klar sieht.
> Vor meinem Fenster
> —sagt der Weise—
> liegt ein Tal,
> darin sammeln sich die Schatten,
> zwei Pappeln säumen einen Weg,
> du weißt—wohin.
>
> Perspektivismus
> ist ein anderes Wort für seine Statik:
> Linien anlegen,
> sie weiterführen
> nach Rankengesetz—
> *Ranken sprühen—,*
> auch Schwärme, Krähen,
> auswerfen in Winterrot von Frühhimmeln,
>
> dann sinken lassen—
>
> du weißt—für wen.
>
> (GW, 3:236)

The poem "Statische Gedichte" (1944) opens with the unusual word "Entwicklungsfremdheit." Benn associates the wisdom of the sage not with disdain for development but with imperviousness to it.[1] The poem conflates the poet and the wise man of Stoic philosophy: both incorporate the virtues of ἀπάθεια ("absence of passion"), ἀταραξία ("unperturbedness"), and αὐτάρχεια ("independence"). The sage, in

Benn's reading, is indifferent to the social and communal order, which seems to concern itself with insignificant affairs. In the reference to children and children's children Benn associates development—as he did in "Wer allein ist—"—with the material sphere of biological reproduction. While the intellect remains static, the material world changes. The repetition in the phrase "Kinder und Kindeskinder" implies, however, that this change and apparent development might easily be reduced to continuation of the same. Traditionally, children are symbols of original innocence and future greatness. In the three metamorphoses of Nietzsche's *Also sprach Zarathustra* children represent motion, a new beginning, a yes to life (2:293–94). The sage, by being impervious to children, is beyond not only the material but also the temporal world.[2] Development and the setting of goals, be they valid or invalid, do not interest him, nor do the intersubjective relations that result in children. Material, evolutionary, and intersubjective concerns appear shallow in comparison with the depth of the sage's own singularly ahistorical and asocial wisdom.

In the second strophe stillness is not just a psychological ideal but an epistemological one as well. The wise man knows; he sees clearly. The world that fails to achieve such wisdom is represented, first, by the adoption of positions—battling for one side against another; second, by action—doing one thing and necessarily not doing another; and third, by travel—literally, from here to there and back, and figuratively, through the development of time. The modern world is in motion and desirous of ends; it undergoes constant metamorphosis and believes in progress. "Richtungen vertreten" suggests, in general, a firm concern with goals; and in particular, active participation in the political process. The world that fails to see clearly is embroiled in finite, political clashes. The sage's stillness and imperviousness to progress preclude all action, which to him must appear mindless, directionless, and meaningless.

The twentieth-century negation of intellect and glorification of those secondary virtues such as discipline, loyalty, and sacrifice which help bring about concrete results in history originated in part from the sense that intellect—specifically, a Nietzschean intellect—serves to undermine the validity of all values, such that we must either avoid reason and embrace primitive life or acknowledge that insofar as all actions are equally invalid they also become, in a perverse sense, equally legitimate.[3] Both positions helped pave the way for the national socialist elevation of action. In addition, socioeconomic and political factors conduced to the twentieth-century distrust of intellect: population growth and rapid urbanization, increasing industrialization, world war and national humiliation, a series of devastating economic crises, the chaos of a democracy unable to protect itself, all undermined the German's faith in an intellectually ordered and stable world. The resulting tendencies were either blind activism—the sense that one can *will* a new order—or withdrawal, the desire to isolate oneself from historical upheaval and disarray.[4] Benn, in distancing himself from the national socialist option, abandons activism entirely: "Nur nicht handeln! Wisse das und schweige. Asien ist tiefer" (GW, 2:151).[5] It is a long way from Fichte's optimistic "Handeln! Handeln! das ist es, wozu wir da sind" (6:345) to Benn's withdrawal from a world in which action can mean only the perversion of intellect. Benn rejects Western culture's embrace of development and glorification of action for the depth and stability of wisdom—Asiatic or Stoic.[6] In his abandonment of goals the poet dismisses all responsibility for the course of the world. The transformation of ideas into action is not only undesirable, it is impossible: "Verwirklichung von Geist im Leben ist nicht mehr" (GW, 2:145). Benn admits of no absolute truths for which he would sacrifice his idyllic existence. All positions relativize each other, except of course the sage's recognition of this relativism and his insight into the futility of all action.[7] Reminiscent of the passive observer and poet depicted in "Wer allein ist—" and of the disconcern for history in "Statische Gedichte" is the passage of Benn's radio dialogue "Können Dichter die Welt ändern?" in which he states that the poet "sieht zu, der weiß, daß der schuldlose Jammer der Welt niemals durch Fürsorgemaßnahmen behoben, niemals durch materielle Verbesserungen überwunden werden kann" (GW, 4:216–17).

There is a complex, even contradictory, tension in "Statische Gedichte" between the fatalist suggestion that history cannot and should not be altered and the poem's unambiguous critique of a particular view of history and implicit call for change, albeit change in the direction of stillness. Benn does not just proffer a general critique of enlightenment optimism and modern disorientation, he directs his comments quite specifically at the national socialist *Bewegung*. "Statische Gedichte" counters the National Socialists' condemnation of *Statik*, their antiintellectualism, their elevation of heroic action and historical destiny along with their exaltation of the collective, of youth, and of the future. The poem is not just an open-ended affirmation of withdrawal and negation of history; it endorses withdrawal as the negation of a particular moment in history. I will not marshal detailed evidence for this historical reading of the poem until my later section on "*Statik* and Inner Emigration": in part because the evidence is multifarious and would take us on too long a digression, in part because the connection between stasis and the critique of national socialist ideology illuminates more than this one poem alone. At this point I would merely suggest that stasis implies not only an abandonment of history and a negation of change but also the negation of a particular form of history—namely, the national socialist elevation of change, action, and movement. As such, it is a call for change in the direction of all that is anathema to change.

Before we return to a detailed reading of the poem, we might briefly consider another tension, though I view this tension as paradoxical, rather than contradictory: the tension between the poem's rootedness in history and its timeless references to action, development, and wisdom. This timeless element invites one to read the poem independently of its historical origins, which can in part be done—first, because the poem's abstractions encourage it; and second, because the poem's reaction to, and critique of, the historical present conduce to an evocation of the timeless. The poem, as we shall see, is both transcendent and contingent.

In German letters, travel is often linked with education—as, for example, in the concept of a *Bildungsreise*. Travel implies an encounter with the particularities of different cultures, with historical traditions. The sage, in contrast, would learn by turning his gaze inward. In true Stoic fashion (more on this later) the sage prefers to rest at home and travel only in his mind. He lives in the country, not the bustling city. His window overlooks a valley, an idyllic image of contentment. Already the view from the window suggests a narrowing of perspective, "einen Ausschnitt aus dem Leben," to cite a parallel formulation of Benn's (*B*, 36). The valley, the shadows, and the poplar trees evoke images of the *locus amoenus*. Shadows, particularly of the poplar tree, are a frequent topos of idyllic poetry—as, for example, in Vergil's *Georgics*, Horace's second Epode, Opitz's "Lob des Feldtlebens," or Hölderlin's "Andenken" (2:188–89). The poet seems less concerned with the direction of the path (its *Richtung*) than with its having a border. The image of a beautiful spot for contemplation and inspiration unites the tradition of psychological-moral *Gemütsruhe* with aesthetic stillness: by removing himself from the distractions and vices of the city, the poet can find the repose and centeredness necessary for creation. The valley suggests both depth and fertility of mind. The path, which leads to no determinate destination, evokes images of idyllic stillness. It is not the path to some heroic endeavor that would take the self out of its solitude. The reference to a *wohin*—one that is never answered, never given specificity—is conceivably ironic. The path simply encircles the valley, and the stanza's vision is atemporal.

But there is a secondary reading of these lines. Perhaps the poet is not immersed in the valley but rather looks down on it from the heights of his insight. The shadows, no longer idyllic, become the negative principle opposed to his enlightenment. Filled with shadows, the valley resembles the depths of Plato's cave. What the poet seeks is not the shadows but the essence, not the ephemeral but the eternal. In this reading of Plato and his doctrine of ἀνάμνησις,[8] Benn can exhibit his lack of concern for the historical. The path is now headed downward, perhaps to death, the ultimate image of transience (and, in a sense, of stasis as well). One remembers that in antiquity the leaves of the poplar tree were used to cloak the dead.[9] The nonanswer to the question of where the path leads might be said to support both readings, but a look at parallel passages lends still further support to the second reading. In three poems, "Entwurzelungen" (GW, 3:118), "Epilog 1949" (GW, 3:345), and "Die Heimat nie—" (GW, 3:411), the phrase "Du weißt" is a gravestone epitaph and signifies knowledge of death. The *Ruhe* of the valley becomes a kind of graveyard stillness. The poet knows the futility not only of action but of all life that is not centered on the locus of eternity: wisdom and poetry. What unites the divergent readings is the concept of limit or perspective. The limit in the first reading is spatial; the idyllic horizon enhances reflection. In the second reading the limit is temporal; awareness of death implies knowledge of the transiency of all life, and thus encourages focused reflection on what is eternal.

Perspectivism is a Nietzschean word,[10] and Benn's poem contains much that reminds the reader of Nietzsche. The connection between stillness and wisdom recalls Nietzsche's description of Apollo's "weisheitsvolle Ruhe" (1:23). Moreover, the poet's disinterest in history makes his postion a combination of what the early Nietzsche calls the unhistorical and the suprahistorical:[11] while the unhistorical individual simply lives with a limited horizon, the suprahistorical individual looks away from progress and focuses on what gives endurance to life, above all, art.[12] The poet wants to return to the permanence he associates with art. The sage, who lives quietly, sees clearly, has wisdom—so too the poet, the artist. For Benn, in fact, art alone assumes the position of purveyor of the absolute, which for Hegel belonged in ascending order to art, religion, and philosophy, and which for the early Nietzsche still encompassed art and religion. In *Weinhaus Wolf* Benn contrasts persons of action and persons of depth; the latter are not philosophers but artists (GW, 2:139). The philosophical world of the philosopher has been subsumed under the guise of aesthetics. The wise man is the poet.

Nietzsche's perspectivism, associated less with stable truth than with motion and the shifting of values, teaches the relativity of all perspectives. Our positions are illusions and might at any moment easily be different. Perspectivism suggests that truth can be reduced to arbitrary moments of our own subjectivity and historicity. Indeed, Nietzsche encourages us to continually overcome our current perspectives in the name of vitality and change. Benn's perspectivism still implies the illusory nature of finite truth ("Richtungen vertreten," etc.), but his position nonetheless differs from Nietzsche's. Benn suggests that we abandon the fluctuating truths that rule our lives and turn to the one locus of stability: poetic wisdom. With his allusion to perspectivism he would place the poet, not in the tradition of Nietzschean relativism and flux, but rather in the much older, less apparent tradition of perspective as the representation of reality (and truth), even from a point of limited and stationary orientation.[13] The sage or poet sees what is essential; what is not essential recedes from the eye, diminishing in size and importance.

The poet draws contours out of his own self "nach Rankengesetz": he carefully lays out and plots the borders of his existence, extending them like tendrils or feelers, in a circular fashion. Out of the kernel of his self, which might again be said to include the various *Schichtungen* of mankind, he is forming words that will express and envelop this kernel. Where "Linien anlegen" and "sie weiterführen" imply careful, constructive work, "Ranken sprühen" suggests a less conscious, more inspirational moment.[14] Benn italicizes the seemingly neglected moment of inspiration. The poem is not the mapping out of logical categories recognized by the sage; it is an *aesthetic* construct. If in "Trunkene Flut" stillness was veiled behind a comprehensive dynamism, in "Statische Gedichte" it is movement ("Ranken sprühen") that takes a subordinate, if still legitimate, position in relation to an overarching stasis. Construction and inspiration overlap not only in the creation of the poem but also in the poet's specific use of the metaphor *Ranken*. With its envelopment of construction and spontaneity as well as its circularity, *Ranken* implies self-sufficiency and wholeness.[15] The poet sprays his tendrils, runners, climbers, shoots, then lets them fall. He has made a poem. One is reminded of Benn's well-known formulation: "Kunst ist der gelungene Ausgleich zwischen Zentrum und Peripherie" (B, 104). The poem is dynamic (note the five verbs of motion in this stanza), but also centripetal.

The poet's circular motion ends with a product that would transcend time. Unlike the philosopher Nietzsche with his desire to express a will that *serves* life, Benn adopts a perspectivism that would enable him to *transcend* life.[16] Another turn away from Nietzsche comes in the poet's use of the word *Krähen*, a central image in Nietzsche's well-known poem "Vereinsamt," from which Benn quotes in other contexts.[17] The third stanza of Nietzsche's poem reads:

> Die Welt—ein Tor
> Zu tausend Wüsten stumm und kalt!
> Wer das verlor,
> Was du verlorst, macht nirgends Halt.

The poem concludes with an image of depravity, the loss of stability, orientation, and community:

> Die Krähen schrein
> Und ziehen schwirren Flugs zur Stadt:
> Bald wird es schneien,—
> Weh dem, der keine Heimat hat!

For Benn, the poet is just as impervious to degeneration as he is to development. The sage's solitude, his lack of a home in the world, seems not to threaten his existence; on the contrary. In a further reversal of Nietzsche's model, the crows are let out and they return. There is in "Statische Gedichte" neither progress nor decay. Disregard for progress and temporality is further expressed through the juxtaposition of *Winterrot*, implying death and decay, and *Frühhimmeln*, a suggestion of dawn and new adventure. The two images cancel one another. The poem invites us to think, not of linear development, whether progressive or regressive, but of the images of return and stasis, roundedness. The poem rejects the apparent linearity of the person of action and history and replaces it with circularity and depth, concepts that Benn frequently links.[18]

"Statische Gedichte" concludes with words that return the reader to the poem's center: "du weißt." The formal structure of repetition and return parallels the poem's disregard for progress. The final "für wen" echoes the ambiguous "wohin." The one person recognized as knowledgeable is of course the poet or sage. The poem, then, is directed not outward—it has no sense of other or of history—but back toward its creator. The phrase "sinken lassen" suggests movement directed not historically downward but privately inward.[19] The "du" in "du weißt" is the wise poet, as is the seemingly nebulous "wen." The poet is his own audience. He can reach for the heavens ("Frühhimmeln"), but he would do so only for himself. Almost as if commenting on this poem's narrowing of perspective and its element of closure, Benn writes in *Doppelleben*: "der Kreis ist in mir beschlossen, ich blicke nicht über mich hinaus" (GW, 4:166).[20]

5. "Reisen"

Reisen

Meinen Sie Zürich zum Beispiel
sei eine tiefere Stadt,
wo man Wunder und Weihen
immer als Inhalt hat?

Meinen Sie, aus Habana,
weiß und hibiskusrot,
bräche ein ewiges Manna
für Ihre Wüstennot?

Bahnhofstraßen und Rueen,
Boulevards, Lidos, Laan—
selbst auf den Fifth Avenueen
fällt Sie die Leere an—

Ach, vergeblich das Fahren!
Spät erst erfahren Sie sich:
bleiben und stille bewahren
das sich umgrenzende Ich.

(GW, 3:327)

"Reisen" (1950) opens with two questions addressed to a stranger or group of strangers. *Wunder* and *Weihen* directly refer to the wonders of travel, but they derive from a religious realm; travel and religion are mutually undermined as forms of diversion that take attention away from the self. The second stanza continues the critique of religion and travel. The two adjectives *weiß* and *hibiskusrot* are placed after the noun they modify. The syntax, together with the stark and increasingly intense contrast between accented and unaccented syllables, conveys to the reader that the speaker is quickly moving toward an answer.[1] *Manna*, the food God gave the people of Israel, is transformed into a twentieth-century context: the modern self hungers for the exotic as a filler for the emptiness of the self. The poetic "you" would leave, not the desert of Egypt, but the *Wüstennot* of the psyche. The goal is not a religious pilgrimage but its modern counterpart, a tourist's travels to famous and exotic lands. *Manna*, relieved of its transcendent implications, becomes purely material—something for the physical, not the psychic, self.[2] Though the poet might seem to abandon religion with his ironization of *Wunder, Weihen,* and *Manna,* the word *Wüste* returns him to a religious context, to the tradition of German mysticism.

In Nietzsche's poem "Vereinsamt," quoted in the previous chapter, we saw that *Wüste* implies the emptiness of a subject at loss in a world that is void of intellectual nourishment or stability. *Wüste,* however, has another, positive meaning. Meister Eckhart calls the center of the soul into which the Godhead enters a "wüeste":[3] "Dirre vunke . . . wil in den einvaltigen grunt, in die stillen wüeste, dâ nie underscheit îngeluogete weder vater noch sun noch heiliger geist . . . dirre grunt ist ein einvaltic stille, diu in ir selben unbewegelich ist, und von dirre unbewegelicheit werdent beweget alliu dinc" (*DW,* 2:419–21). Benn was familiar with this mystical reading of the word *Wüste.* In *Der Ptolemäer* he specifically refers to Eckhart and his concept of "die 'stille Wüste der Gottheit' " (*GW,* 2:222).[4] Angelus Silesius, who also stands in the tradition of German mysticism, likewise describes the Godhead (and ideal soul) as a desert: "Jch muß noch über GOtt in eine wůste ziehn" (1:7). For the mystics, the stillness or emptiness of the desert soul is a necessary condition for union with God and ultimate self-fulfillment. In this stillness God speaks to us. Eckhart writes: "In der stille und in der ruowe . . . da sprichet got in die sêle und sprichet sich alzemâle in die sêle" (*DW,* 1:317); and in another passage he asserts: "ibi est quies et silentium, ubi pater loquitur verbum" ("there is quiet and silence, where the Father speaks the word" [*LW,* 4:228, my translation]).[5] Travel and tradition lead away from the self; rootedness, mysticism, and stillness lead back to the self. In his "Epilog und lyrisches Ich" Benn writes of his own strong desire for a desert, which, however, is not available to him through travel: "immer wieder . . . ging ich auf Reisen, immer wieder mußte ich zurück, da ich in Europa keine Wüste fand" (*GW,* 4:10). The "you" in the poem is being challenged in regard to the belief that an exploration of the depths and wonders of life requires a confrontation with the unusual, the exotic, the distant. By emptying out of the self all false concerns and leaving only a desert, the self is ready to receive truth. In Benn's "Verlorenes Ich," the self loses itself in a world of objectivity, externality, and technology, a realm from which religion and mystical meaning have disappeared; in "Reisen" the self comes to itself and its mystical dimensions by isolating a sphere of private, subjective, spiritual enclosure.

Though the poem objects to literal travel, it does evoke a kind of intellectual journey. Zurich and Havana might initially be viewed as parallel: both travel destinations, they are introduced with religious rhetoric; each is associated, directly or indirectly, with red and white imagery; and finally, each gives a nonanswer to the dilemmas of the modern self. Reflection on the two cities tells us only what the poet is *not* offering as a solution. The two stanzas present us with a message *ex negativo*, or a *via negationis*. In this sense the travel-motif is reinvoked, as a journey of the mind, a dominant structure in the mystic tradition—as, for example, in Bonaventure's *Itinerarium Mentis in Deum*. Counseling against distractions and concupiscence, Bonaventure, like Benn, asks the reader to enter into the self as a means by which to reach stillness and immutability. Benn of course stops at the self and does not pass beyond it, as does a religious thinker like Bonaventure. For Bonaventure, God is center and circumference; for Benn, center and circumference are occupied by the self-limiting subject. Benn's journey is secularized and could be described as an inward path that avoids not only dispersive travel but also what is associated with religious spirituality and exotic sensuality.

Zurich and Havana, though in many respects parallel, can also be viewed as opposites. The religious rhetoric of the first stanza serves to reawaken for the listener the religious associations of Zurich, namely Zwingli and Calvinism.[6] In contrast, Havana, with its tropical climate, evokes a world of the flesh.[7] This association is reinforced by the inversion of *Manna* as well as by the term *hibiskusrot*, which has decidedly sensual and sexual implications. Neither religious spiritualism, as evoked by the older city, Zurich, nor sensual materialism, associated with the newer city, Havana, is Benn's answer. Rather, the poem endorses secularized reflection on the locus of the self, as developed by the modern prophet, the poet. The two cities and their associations are introduced, no less than the religious rhetoric, only to be discarded and overcome.

Since every element in a poem should be weighed for its potential meaning,[8] one is tempted to pursue in greater detail the question, Why Zurich?[9] Several hypotheses beyond the religious associations come to mind. Zurich is located in a neutral country, where, it is easy to imagine, everything must be in harmony. The references to depth and wonder may evoke Zurich as the city of Carl Jung. In addition, Zurich has the most famous of all *Bahnhofstraßen*, and it is the city of the new and outrageous, the Dada movement. Though the poem as poem invites these kinds of associations, the particular context would seem to undermine such a search. First, Zurich is hardly an ideal: it does not represent depth or create wonder, it only appears to do so; the *Bahnhofstraßen* are seen to be insignificant. Many cities fail to give the self precisely what Zurich cannot offer; one recalls the simple but telling words "zum Beispiel." Second, the thrust of the first two stanzas is toward the arbitrariness of the tourist's travels; the selection of Zurich may mirror this process. In fact if Zurich were chosen because of Dada, the choice would appear contradictory: Dada is ruled by the laws of chance. Finally, the rhythm of the poem takes us from the arbitrary content of travel to the poet's affirmation of the self; "Zurich" finds its truth in the poem's final word, "Ich." This reading of Zurich suggests that the city was selected not only because of the above associations, and not only because it contains the word *Ich* and thus allows for a playful association with the self, but also because the city contrasts with—and veils, even as it contains—the self. In German "Zurich" is written "Zürich": it is thus twice removed from the self—first, by way of the wrong gender, and second, by way of the umlaut. Even from a linguistic standpoint, travel does not lead "toward the self." The poet's choice of Zurich, the one city that ends with "ich," appears, like much in Benn, above all formal. However, the play on "Zür-ich," along with the earlier connections, does reveal that the choice is meaningful; it becomes in a complex way both arbitrary and significant.

Though the poem affirms the private stillness of the self, it does not suggest that one leave the restless city for its other—for, let's say, the country. The poem differs in this way from "Statische Gedichte," at least from a particular reading of that poem.[10] If disorientation were restricted to city life, one could travel to the country or to foreign lands, to Cuba, for example, and escape chaos; but "Reisen" undermines this option. The city's restlessness serves as a metaphor for the general disorientation of modern individuals, who, independent of location, have no objective structure—no "-ism," as it were—to guide their lives. The Nietzschean sense of *Wüste*, though overridden by our primary reading, is still apparent. The modern self, in its *Wüstennot*, is at the juncture of meaninglessness and self-realization. While the poem seems to open with a series of gestures to the world, the first two stanzas serve mainly to bring us back to our own selves. What is significant is not the geography or history of the world, not its spiritual or sensual attractions, but the solitude and strength of the individual. Though "Reisen" may be said to counter the affirmation of idyllic existence in "Statische Gedichte," this later poem nonetheless upholds Benn's view of perspectivism as knowledge located in the subject's particular view of the world.

In the third stanza motion becomes ever more hectic. Streets are named in languages from around the world.[11] The poet, while apparently not speaking from extensive experience (the reliability of which is undermined in the course of the poem), nonetheless seems to imply that his message is somehow universal. Within this motion, confusion, and mass of people—the streets named are for the most part busy ones: *Bahnhofstraßen*, for example, which suggest even further travel, and Fifth Avenues—there is emptiness.[12] Even in the world's liveliest city the void is present. The lack of direction—the sequence seems random—must be read symbolically, ideologically. Motion creates a chaotic emptiness, and this void not only threatens and invades the self ("fällt Sie die Leere an"), it seems to crash in upon the strophe.[13] The poet implies—almost in the language of contemporary existentialism—that instead of diffusing one's attention and experiencing a flood of images, it is necessary to concentrate on the stillness of one's own conscience or consciousness and listen to the desert or nothingness of the self before reaching an awareness of authentic selfhood. Negating both travel and the contemporary tendency to occupy oneself with whatever is current, Benn writes in another context: "wer mit der Zeit mitläuft, wird von ihr überrannt, aber wer stillsteht, auf den kommen die Dinge zu" (GW, 1:428).[14] Stillness brings an emptiness from which the self surfaces intact and in which meaning, however mysterious, is revealed: "Die Leere ist wohl auch von jenen Gaben, / in denen sich der Dunkle offenbart" (GW, 3:252).

By conceiving of travel as a failed attempt to flee from the self, Benn again aligns himself with Stoic tradition. As Seneca said of the wealthy Romans who took trips in order to escape their problems, the psychic self always travels along with the physical self.[15] In his twenty-eighth letter Seneca writes that one needs "a change of character, not climate": "How can novelty of surroundings abroad and becoming acquainted with foreign scenes or cities be of any help? All that dashing about turns out to be quite futile. And if you want to know why all this running away cannot help you, the answer is simply this: you are running away in your own company. You have to lay aside the load on your spirit. Until you do that, nowhere will satisfy you."[16] In his 104th letter Seneca adds that the sights of exotic places hold our attention only momentarily, much as children wonder at the unfamiliar. In the long run the motion of travel only increases the restlessness of a troubled mind:

> What good has travel of itself ever been able to do anyone? . . . All it has ever done is distract us for a little while, through the novelty of our surroundings, like children fascinated by something they haven't come across before. The instability, moreover,

of a mind which is seriously unwell, is aggravated by it, the motion itself increasing the fitfulness and restlessness. This explains why people, after setting out for a place with the greatest enthusiasm, are often more enthusiastic about getting away from it; like migrant birds, they fly on, away even quicker than they came.[17]

In both Seneca's reading and Benn's, problems cannot be overcome through travel, through merely physical change.

The last stanza unambiguously states what the slightly ironic tone and the increasingly intense questioning have implied: travel and experience are of no help to the individual seeking identity; one must look inward. The poem addresses not an intimate *du* but a distanced *Sie*. The *Sie* conveys depersonalization and lack of involvement; it signifies a break from the tradition of *Erlebnislyrik*, with its stress on intersubjective relations and the self's desire to experience the world. The distance created by the use of *Sie* corresponds to the poem's message: create a border between self and world so that you can reflect on the self. "Reisen" appears as a poem of distance, not intimacy. Toward the end of the poem, however, the tone shifts: with the word "Ach" the poet abandons any pretense of poetic indifference toward the issue at hand.[18] The use of "Ach" has an additional purpose: it invites the reader to compare "Reisen" with another famous poem on travel, Eichendorff's "Sehnsucht," in which we find at the close of the first stanza the suggestive lines, "Ach, wer da mitreisen könnte / In der prächtigen Sommernacht" (21).[19] The Romantic longing for the unity of self and world, the enchanting idea of exotic, meaningful travel is broken by Benn, who suggests, rather than movement into the world, a stationary and self-sufficient closure. Benn's elegiac "Ach" refers not to lost travel but to time lost through travel.

In this final stanza Benn sets up a series of etymological relations. Travel ("Fahren") and experience ("Erfahren") are juxtaposed. Originally, to *experience* the world meant not simply to perceive or become aware of the world but to *travel*. Benn implies that the etymology reveals an error in world view. Travel has little to do with true experience.[20] One frequently associates a frontier or *Grenze* with travel. Odysseus, for example, traveled to the outer limits of the world. Benn counters with the concept of a self-limiting subject: "das sich umgrenzende Ich." The *Grenze* becomes not the frontier of outer lands, but the limits and properties of one's own self. The self comes to itself through the recognition of its own limit ($πέρας$), not through travel and experience (ἐμπειρία); the poem's etymological play is not restricted to German. As in the early cultural criticism of the Rönne stories, here too the empirical world, the world of collecting experiences and facts, the world of pure activity, lacks meaning.[21] The self's recognition of this comes late—presumably when external circumstances, rather than inner awareness, bring the self out of a world of dispersion and travel and toward solitude and reflection. Typical of Benn's disdain for action, the last two lines of the poem avoid the use of the finite verb.

Benn's position vis-à-vis travel is not unique, even within the German tradition. Adalbert Stifter, the most diligent of nineteenth-century spokesmen for stillness, lets the hero of his novel *Der Nachsommer* come to himself—and the reader to his name—not after extended travels to remote parts of the continent, but after repeated visits to a single location. The narrator treats Heinrich Drendorf's eventual *Bildungsreise* in just two paragraphs of a novel that lasts a good 700 pages.[22] Heinrich's development unfolds in an almost still-life atmosphere.[23] The narrative technique of circling back to elements previously introduced and presenting them in ever-new light, rather than racing on to novel adventures, reinforces this point, as does the work's self-reflexive elevation of aesthetic stillness, particularly in Risach's discussion of the marble statue.[24] Benn was of course familiar with Stifter's text.[25]

Any poem in German literature that ends with the word "Ich" invites comparison with Goethe's "Prometheus" (1:44–46). Benn's "Ich" is not the powerful and outwardly rebellious self of Goethe's poem, but he is a rebel: first, against religion, insofar as it directs our attention away from the self and toward the otherworldly or the afterlife; and second, against the modern enthusiasm for motion, travel, and materialism. Benn's ego embraces restrictions and finite limits; not so Prometheus, whose concept of self encompasses the entire earth. The poetic rhythm mirrors this deviation from the Titanism of Goethe's poem: the metric stress lies not with the self but with the concept of a limit. The *Grenze*, however, is conveyed in a slightly ambiguous light. It may be a strong marker that confidently asserts the stability of the self, or it may be a defensive border, a mode of escapist withdrawal. For Seneca the self that is at peace with itself does not seek travel but nonetheless remains tranquil even when it finds itself in the busiest of surroundings: "Could there be a scene of greater turmoil than the Forum? Yet even there, if need be, you are free to lead a life of peace."[26] Benn's self, on the other hand, seems to require a physical distance from the world. The ambiguity of the limit—a self-assertive marker, or a defense mechanism—is left open.

While the poem's apodictic tone seems to speak for the first reading, the context and lack of assertive stress in the particular line open up the second reading.[27] The nonresolution of the ambiguity implies that the multiplicity of readings must be preserved and viewed together on a higher level: perhaps the poet is himself unsure of his strength, perhaps he is so withdrawn that the reader is by necessity unable to determine the exact contours of his self. Either way, it is clear that Benn's ego is no longer the dynamic "Ich" of Goethe's poem,[28] nor as in Greek mythology the servant of mankind; he is tranquil and withdrawn.[29] The tone of the poem, clear and confident but subdued, the poem, clear and confident but subdued, confirms this point.

Like Prometheus, the poet is a creator. Just as the eighteenth century regarded the poet—in Shaftesbury's famous phrase—as a "second *Maker*; a just Prometheus under Jove" (1:136), so is Benn's poet a second god—not, however, in the tradition of the dynamic Prometheus, but rather in the tradition of Aristotle's unmoved mover.[30] While all around the poet the world is in motion, he himself is still: "bleiben und stille bewahren." The poet is a god not so much in his productivity as in his stillness and self-suffiency. In "Trunkene Flut" the poet also takes on the role of a god: like Christ, he is a great sufferer; in "Reisen," the god is not Christian but Aristotelian,[31] and he is characterized by repose and constancy, not suffering and sacrifice. Aristotle's god is contemplative, not active; while objects around him move, he himself remains motionless. The only motion the poet admits is a motion—the creation of his poem—that does not disturb his inner peace; moreover, he is in need of nothing outside himself.[32] By stressing the proximity of god and poet, of religious and aesthetic self, Benn unites in this poem the two traditions of religious stillness (Aristotelian and mystical) with the concept of aesthetic stillness, just as in "Statische Gedichte" he combines Stoic and aesthetic stillness.

The last line of each stanza is interesting. The first stanza invites speculation as to the content of travel to a foreign city. The middle two stanzas introduce two words for emptiness, *Wüstennot* and *Leere*. Only in the last stanza is a positive category explicitly invoked. The linear movement of travel, represented in the first three stanzas, leads nowhere. The stillness and stability of the self, on the other hand, expressed in the circular imagery of *umgrenzen*, lead to self-fulfillment. The equation of stillness and circularity, with which we first became familiar in our analysis of "Trunkene Flut," has become an image of not only the excellent poem but also the authentic self.[33] The negation of linear thought in "Reisen" is complemented by the return to earlier world views: in particular, the Stoic and mystic stilling of outward activity, and in general, the anti-Faustian embrace of limits.[34] When Benn writes that his "Statische Gedichte" are "anti-faustisch" (*DD*, 93), he implies, at least in part, that they take us back to the Apollinian or Greek principle of the limit, with which Oswald Spengler contrasts the modern, Faustian world of the infinite.[35]

6. *Statik* and Inner Emigration

At the beginning of this study I mentioned my desire to focus on a side of Benn's poetry less known than his shocking and innovative early works, namely his movement toward a concept of formal balance and stillness. I would like to analyze this side of Benn from another angle and illuminate a dimension of his poetry that readers of German literature have consistently overlooked. Nonspecialists, even German scholars, are more likely to know that Benn openly supported the early national socialist regime than that his poetry of the late thirties and early forties might be viewed as a form of inner emigration.[1]

Benn's association with nazism is a biographical fact, evidenced in part by his writings from the first year and a half after Hitler's assumption of power—above all, by his two radio broadcasts "Der neue Staat und die Intellektuellen" and "Antwort an die literarischen Emigranten." The issue of Benn's relationship to nazism has been analyzed most thoroughly by Reinhard Alter,[2] who views Benn's affirmation of the Third Reich as a consequence of primarily two factors: first, his desire for the separation of art and politics—a position he held consistently, which also led, ultimately, to his disassociation from the regime; and second, his misjudgment of the national socialist view of art and politics, which derived in part from his lack of interest in empirical details.[3]

Falsely associating the politicization of art solely with the left, Benn sided with the National Socialists in 1933, believing that they would free art from political influence or purpose. His adulation of the regime was, in this respect, neither forced nor passive. Benn was instrumental in bringing the prestigious Preußische Akademie der Künste, into which he had been accepted in 1932, into alignment with the Nazi regime.[4] He did so, according to Alter, primarily with the intention of preserving the purity of art.

Yet there was more. In national socialism Benn also saw the negation of materialist values, whether capitalist or Marxist (he was, as suggested above, not given to finite distinctions), and the development of a metaphysically oriented view of history.[5] An advantage of nazism as opposed to Marxism was, for Benn, the turn "vom ökonomischen zum mythischen Kollektiv" (*GW*, 1:441). To echo another conservative irrationalist, Moeller van den Bruck, one could say that Prussia-Germany had finally received its myth.[6] Of this myth and its

40 Statik *and Inner Emigration*

metaphysical depth Benn writes: "Welch intellektueller Defekt . . . in diesem allem [the Third Reich] *nicht* das anthropologisch Tiefere zu sehen" (*GW*, 1:440).

In Benn's eyes national socialism became a creative act, something spontaneous and irrational, and in this sense more artistic than political. It was, in Benn's own words, formal. In his preface to "Kunst und Macht," he writes "was wir heute rassenmäßig verlangen, ist *Form*" (*GW*, 4:399). In his "Rede auf Marinetti," he states that this "form" is realized in Italian and German fascism: "die beiden Symbole der neuen Reiche" are "Form und Zucht" (*GW*, 1:481).[7] Benn's comments on the *Führer* reinforce this image of a formally innovative and creative impulse at work in contemporary history:

> Das Neue, Aufrührerische, aber gleichzeitig auch Synthetische der Verwandlung zeigt sich in dem spezifischen Führerbegriff. Führer ist nicht der Inbegriff der Macht, ist überhaupt nicht als Terrorprinzip gedacht, sondern als höchstes geistiges Prinzip gesehen. Führer: das ist das Schöpferische, in ihm sammeln sich die Verantwortung, die Gefahr und die Entscheidung, auch das ganze Irrationale des ja erst durch ihn sichtbar werdenden geschichtlichen Willens, ferner die ungeheure Bedrohung, ohne die er nicht zu denken ist, denn er kommt ja nicht als Muster, sondern als Ausnahme, er beruft sich selbst, man kann natürlich auch sagen, er wird berufen, es ist die Stimme aus dem feurigen Busch, der folgt er, dort muß er hin und besehen das große Gesicht. (*GW*, 1:214–15)

Because Benn recognizes no valid content, the formal transference from chaos to order, from stagnation to creativity, is sufficient criterion for the acceptance of nazism. The everyday concerns of competing political parties disappear before a metaphysical, antiintellectual,[8] antiempirical view of politics. In his preface to "Der neue Staat und die Intellektuellen" Benn writes: "Alles, was heute politisch und empirisch sichtbar wird und Form gewinnt, ist . . . jenseitig, kausallos, transzendent, eine innere Macht stößt in ihr vor" (*GW*, 4:393–94). In heralding the creative irrationalism of the regime he writes, "daß es sich bei den Vorgängen in Deutschland gar nicht um politische Kniffe handelt, die man in der bekannten dialektischen Manier verdrehen und zerreden könnte, sondern es handelt sich um das Hervortreten eines neuen biologischen Typs, die Geschichte mutiert und ein Volk will sich züchten" (*GW*, 4:242). Politics gives way to biology and myth. Benn continues: "es handelt sich hier gar nicht um Regierungsformen, sondern um eine neue Vision von der Geburt des Menschen, vielleicht um eine alte, vielleicht um die letzte großartige Konzeption der weißen Rasse" (*GW*, 4:243). The value of the vision derives not from its coherence but from its formal desirability and its strength. Power renders the party legitimate: "in einem zehnjährigen, öffentlich geführten, vor aller Augen sich abspielenden Kampf haben sie [the National Socialists] gemeinsam das Reich erobert, keine Macht konnte sie hindern, keine Widerstände sie zurückhalten, es war überhaupt keine andere Macht mehr da—, auch hierin zeigt sich das Elementare, Unausweichliche, immer weiter um sich greifend Massive der geschichtlichen Verwandlung" (*GW*, 1:215).

Writing to Gertrud Hindemith in the fall of 1933, Benn describes his choice for national socialism in decisionistic terms:[9]

> Man muß sich entschließen, *Sie* müssen sich entschließen, in den heute vorliegenden Fragen des Volkes u. seiner Regeneration *Grundlegendes* zu sehen. Es hat mit Politik, Schiebung, Wirtschaft nichts zu tun . . . Man *sieht* das jetzt plötzlich so exact, es kommt doch vor, daß sich plötzlich Durchblicke öffnen, neue Einbettungen ergeben u. ob Sie wollen oder nicht: hier ist der letzte Versuch, ein Volk zu regenerieren, ich weiß nicht, ob die angewandten Methoden richtig sind, das bezweifle ich sogar, aber ein bewundernswerter Wille ist doch da . . . Hier ist Stoff u. inneres Erlebnis—ran! Hier ist Geschichte—ertrage sie. Hier ist Schicksal—friß Vogel oder stirb! Gefahren, Untergang—liebe sie! Amor fati—"dennoch die Schwerter halten." (*H*, 67–69)

As the *Führer* is chosen, so the German must also choose. The question of rational criteria is left unaddressed. Instead, Benn calls on an aesthetic sense of experience, the manifestation of will, the nearness to an abyss.

In addition, Benn was attracted to the assertive and authoritarian dimensions of nazism. He praises the new state for being "monistisch, antidialektisch, überdauernd und autoritär" (*GW*, 1:214). The national socialist regime is not to be questioned with arguments or facts. This helps explain Benn's proclivity to overlook contradictions within the program as well as between the program and historical reality. The irrationalism of his view derives in part from his inheritance of Nietzschean historicism. The national socialist movement has brought forth new structures that cannot be judged by the old standards, for these have no transhistorical validity (*GW*, 1:445–46).

As Benn eventually recognized the political thrust of nazism, the same principle that had led him to support the movement motivated him to disavow it.[10] Though he was eager to aestheticize politics, he was not willing to accept a politicized art. National socialism subordinated art to the interests of the state. Benn's sense of priorities differed: form was superior to the state and thus to both propaganda and censorship.[11] Art was subservient not to the state but to totality, to which the state itself was also subservient: "Der totale Staat selbst ist ja ein Abglanz jener Welttotalität, jener substantiellen Einheit aller Erscheinungen und Formen, jener transzendenten Geschlossenheit eines in sich ruhenden Seins, jenes Logos, jener religiösen Ordnung, zu der die Kunst aus sich heraus mit ihren konstruktiven Mitteln, also aus ihrem eigenen aufbauenden, hinreißenden und reinigenden Prinzip unaufhörlich strebt, die sie verwirklicht, die sie überhaupt der Menschheit erst in Erscheinung brachte" (GW, 1:260).

In Benn's turn away from national socialism two moments are thus dominant: first, his consistent belief in the nonpoliticization of art and his slow recognition that the National Socialists would not, any more than the Socialists or Communists, grant him the freedom and legitimacy of pure poetry; second, his disenchantment with specific dimensions of the national socialist program[12] and the eventual rift between his own view of transcendent harmony and his recognition of national socialist reality.[13] These two moments resulted in his returning to an earlier view, according to which spirit should not or cannot be realized in history—not just the national socialist vision of history, but history as such. As early as September 1934, Benn denies in a letter to Ina Seidel the possibility of any unification of "Geist und Macht. Das ist vorbei. Es sind *zwei* Reiche."[14] Benn's negation of nazism is a turn away from history and the public sphere, but it is a turn informed by politics and can be viewed in the context of that part of the resistance known as the inner emigration.

In an enlightening introduction to an anthology of essays on the German resistance, Richard Löwenthal describes three basic types of resistance: political opposition, social refusal, and intellectual dissidence. While the first counters the monopoly of political power and the second the monopoly of social and organizational control, the third attempts to undermine a monopoly of thought. In Germany, political opposition included, for example, the early illegal activities of Communists and trade unions, the leaflet campaign of the "White Rose," and the attempted assassination of 20 July 1944; less direct and open, though in some instances highly effective, was the refusal of institutions and individuals to adhere to the regulations of the regime. The church—the Catholic church more than the Protestant—provides us with instances of social refusal; to a degree one can also consider here the army and the bureaucracy, in the sense that they consciously reacted against the penetration of their ranks by National Socialist intruders or, in individual cases, illegally helped potential victims. Also within the category of social refusal are the activities of non-Nazi youth groups. Independent of any institutional framework, social refusal surfaced in such acts as the illegal reception of foreign radio broadcasts.

Though virtually all opponents of Hitler's regime were also opponents of the national socialist world view, one can speak of cultural dissidence as a third and distinct form of resistance. It is here that the concept "inner emigration" surfaces. Because the more liberal and politically active writers were not tolerated in Germany, the authors of the inner emigration—Rudolf Alexander Schröder, Werner Bergengruen, Reinhold Schneider, and others—tend to fit either a conservative or an apolitical profile. These authors do not present detailed analyses of the contemporary political scene; instead, they focus on universal values that transcend time and space. Their goal was to preserve traditional norms in an intellectual manner at a time when reality denied these norms. Though their efforts had little, if any, direct political effect, the norms they embraced seemed necessary for the reestablishment of a humanistic Germany. The goals, in comparison with most instances of political and social resistance, were modest, but no less compelling for that. In an age where what was timeless gave way to what was expedient and instrumental, the writers of the inner emigration addressed not so much the Third Reich in its social and political dimensions as the moral disorientation and spiritual crisis out of which the Third Reich in part developed and the extent to which national socialism was continuing to undermine and further dismantle the Germans' adherence to traditional values.[15] Benn, with his embrace of stasis, of that which abides, belongs among these writers.[16]

In suggesting that Benn's concept of stasis be viewed as a form of "inner emigration," I recognize the difficulties associated with this term.[17] Extreme positions have been taken with regard to the concept, ranging from Thomas Mann's initial condemnation of anyone who published in Germany during the national socialist era to Frank Thieß's suggestion, adopting a figure of thought ironically not unfamiliar to Mann, that only those who suffered, and indeed suffered in Germany, have the most valuable new insights for Germany and the world.[18] Both positions miss the mark: Mann's insofar as it overlooks the hidden meanings of opposition poetry; Thieß's insofar as it ignores the consistency of the émigrés and bases intellectual and moral truth solely on experience, an antinormative and potentially fascist position.[19] Within the literature of inner emigration one can draw a distinction between non-Nazi poetry—poetry that refuses to deal with the privileged themes of national socialist art (heroic optimism, the call for battle, the cult of the flag and of the nation, the elevation of Germanic blood and of secondary virtues such as loyalty, obedience, sacrifice, and courage)—and anti-Nazi poetry, poetry that directly confronts the positions of the National Socialists.[20] The distinction has some heuristic value, though it is not always clear into which group a work should fall. It is best to draw these distinctions along a spectrum.[21] Benn's static poems are proof of this point: while they do not confront the National Socialists as directly as a work like Jan Petersen's *Unsere Straße*, they are not merely poems that refuse to deal with the prescribed topics of national socialist art. The poems—as I will attempt to demonstrate below—are anti-Nazi, even though the effectiveness of their opposition is limited, first, by their elliptical critique of the movement,[22] and second, by internal deficiencies in the concept of stasis.[23]

The distinctly oppositional connotations of *Statik* can be recognized in three ways: first, in the necessarily political ramifications of a twentieth-century German poetry that views itself as anti-Faustian; second, in Benn's stress on the contrast between *Statik* and *Bewegung* when viewed in the light of national socialist rhetoric; and third, in the function served by such principles as stillness, interiority, and transcendence in Benn's poems of this period, principles embraced by other writers of the inner emigration as well.

In its particularly German reception, the adjective *Faustian* took on nationalist and optimistic connotations, especially during the Second Reich.[24] The nationalist associations persisted into the Nazi era.[25] In his study of the Faustian theme Hans Schwerte notes, for example, a gruesome, if almost amusing, title from 1933: *Faust im Braunhemd* (279).[26] Benn's anti-Faustian poetry is by definition a negation of political (and nationalist) optimism. His "Wer allein ist—" subordinates a Heraclitean-Faustian view of the world to a position that embraces stillness and emotionlessness. Geological stability stands fast against the volcanic and eruptive forces of both nature and history; the dynamic elements of Goethe, his "Stirb und Werde," give way to a stasis that is openly anti-Faustian. The *Entwicklungsfremdheit* of Benn's "Statische Gedichte" likewise counters notions of historical destiny and inevitable progression into the future. Moreover, it opposes the Titanism of striving and action,[27] of great deeds, and ultimately—in the national socialist reading of *Faust*—the hero of the *Gemeinschaft*.

Benn's criticism of the Faustian present becomes explicit in his essay "Zum Thema Geschichte," where he writes of the ruthless acts of his contemporaries in their search for external salvation:

> Sehr verdächtig in dieser Richtung ist der Erlösungsgedanke, der ihre Musik- und Bühnendramen durchzieht. Tannhäuser und seine Variationen, Fliegender Holländer, Parsifal, nicht "Faust", aber die faustischen Motive—: erst benehmen sie sich wie die Schweine, dann wollen sie erlöst werden. Von irgendeiner "höheren" Macht, die ihnen ihr tumbes, stures Weben und Wabern vergibt. Sie kommen gar nicht darauf, sich selber durch einen Gedanken innerer Erziehung, durch Einfügen in ein Moralprinzip oder eine prophylaktische Vernunft in Ordnung zu halten oder wieder in Form zu bringen, sie haben ihre "Dränge", das ist faustisch—und dann wollen sie erlöst werden. (GW, 1:376)

Benn suggests that the Faustian impulse be tempered with self-denial, self-discipline, and moderation, that the national socialist present be countered with inwardness, morality, reason, or form. "Statische Gedichte" and the later "Reisen" negate reckless action and recognize that salvation must come from within; both imply the need for moderation; both embrace the order of form and the value of self-restraint. These works, together with "Wer allein ist—," override the tendency toward dynamism that we saw in "Trunkene Flut." The embrace of *Grenze* in the later "Reisen" is, moreover, a thematic extension of Benn's elevation of thought in "Wer allein ist—" and "Statische Gedichte," a position he associates with his own anti-Faustianism. The promotion of limits is stylistic, but not only stylistic:

> Nur der darf zugelassen werden zum Denken, der diese ungeheuerliche Kraft einer einzigen späten, massenmäßig geringen Art auch durch die äußerst erreichbare Formulierung, die gespannteste Wendung bändigt und stählern begrenzt, der das Gefühl hat für diese Grenze und die Ergebenheit vor dieser Grenze. Es ist wie in der Kunst. Der äußerst erreichbare Ausdruck muß erkämpft und gehalten werden mit einer Schärfe, die aufs rücksichtsloseste alles teilt und scheidet, aber man muß wissen, ob man zu weiteren Formulierungen noch berufen ist. Verliert man den Instinkt hierfür, wird man titanisch . . . man wird rückfällig in die . . . infantile faustische Welt. (GW, 4:61)

The anti-Faustian element not only undermines nationalist optimism and reinforces a stylistic and thematic elevation of clarity and re-

46 Statik and Inner Emigration

straint, it conveys to us the broad interdisciplinary connotations of *Statik*. The one writer who did the most for the revival of the Faustian motif in early twentieth-century Germany was Oswald Spengler. As I suggested in the last chapter, Spengler contrasts Faustian boundlessness, expansion, and dynamism with Apollinian closure, restraint, and "Statik" (234). The terms were available to Benn; he had only to develop them.

There can be no doubt that Benn's selection of the term *Statik* as a specifically twentieth-century form of stillness was due not solely to its scientific connotations. Not long after the fall of the Third Reich Benn writes: "Natürlich wird schon allein der Titel '*Statische* Gedichte' Anstoß erregen in einer Zeit, die sich in einer—wenn auch sinnlosen—Bewegung zu befinden als ihr besonderes Verdienst u. ihre politische Forderung ansieht" (emphasis in the original, Oelze no. 315 [12 September 1946]). *Statik* was a highly charged concept within national socialism itself. In *Der Mythus des 20. Jahrhunderts*, a work Benn owned,[28] Alfred Rosenberg, the major philosopher of national socialism,[29] introduces *Statik* and *Bewegung* as two of his leitmotifs. He proposes "zwei Arten des Lebensgefühls: *dynamisches Wesen oder statische Wertsetzung*" (emphasis in the original, 126).[30] In the course of his numerous allusions to *Statik* Rosenberg speaks disparagingly of a "statische Weltbetrachtung" (127), "das statische Weltbild" (133), "das statische Ideal" (134), "plastische Statik" (305), and "die Sehnsucht . . . nach Ruhe, nach Statik und Monismus" (323).

Rosenberg links *Statik* with Greek, Jewish, Christian, and Asian world views. In his discussion of Greek culture he focuses on "die *Statik* des griechischen Lebens" (emphasis in the original, 151). Stasis is monistic and stagnant, the realm of eternal, universal truth to which Rosenberg contrasts the Northern, dynamic notion of race. Greek culture cannot compete with contemporary Germany's dynamism: "*Das artbedingte Schöne als äußere Statik der nordischen Rasse, das ist Griechentum, das arteigene Schöne als innere Dynamik, das ist nordisches Abendland*" (emphasis in the original, 293). Greek beauty is static, not dynamic.[31] Even Greek literature borders on the stillness of sculpture (305), whereas Germanic art, even its architecture, is dynamic and Faustian (351–52). In a distinctly anti-Semitic passage Rosenberg speaks of "die fremde Statik alles Jerusalemitischen" (130), and he contrasts the Jewish and Christian world views with Northern dynamism: "Diese statische Selbstbehauptung ist der metaphysische Grund für des Juden Zähigkeit und Stärke, aber auch für seine absolute kulturelle Unfruchtbarkeit und sein schmarotzerhaftes Wirken . . . Diese triebhafte Statik bildet auch das Rückgrat der römischen

Kirche" (128). Meister Eckhart, who is more German than Christian, is praised for his defiance of stasis: "An Stelle der jüdisch = römischen Statik setzt er die Dynamik der nordisch = abendländischen Seele" (252).[32] *Statik* is also related to the inferior, Asian world: "Die Freude an Lao = tses Weisheit ist die Sehnsucht nach einem seelischen und geistigen Gegenpol. Sie ist aber keine Übereinstimmung und nichts ist falscher, als uns die Weisheit des Ostens als auch uns gemäß oder gar als eine uns überlegene zu preisen, wie es müde und innerlich rhythmenlos gewordene Europäer heute zu tun belieben" (264-65). Rosenberg adds: "Hier stehen wir denn vor der Frage, ob diese scheinbar schöne große Ruhe des Chinesen nicht eine innere Regungslosigkeit der Seele bedeutet, nur die Kehrseite des wenig lebendigen Inneren" (266-67). Just as Rosenberg contrasts Germanic activity with Jewish restlessness, so does he set Germanic centeredness apart from Asiatic peace: "die Ruhe Goethes ist nicht die Ruhe Lao = tses und die Tat Bismarcks ist nicht die Tätigkeit Rothschilds. Die germanische Persönlichkeit hat nicht ein Stück von chinesischer Ruhe und ein Stückchen jüdischer Geschäftigkeit" (266).[33]

According to Rosenberg, Germanic art should embody the Nordic "Kraft des Heroisch = Willenhaften," which is to be found in figures such as Siegfried and Faust (434). Rosenberg calls this active, heroic principle that ideally dominates both creativity and reception "aesthetic will."[34] He contrasts it with the Greek ideal of *Ruhe* and the Kantian concept of disinterested contemplation: "Es entsteht dann der Lehrsatz von der 'willenlosen Kontemplation,' gefolgt von der Leugnung des aesthetischen Willens. Der griechische Mythus der Harmonie und gewollten Ruhe überschattete den germanischen Instinkt, den Anlauf zum kraftvollen Selbstbekenntnis und auch künstlerischer Willensentladung" (320). In Greece and later in classical Germany the willful act of creation gave way to "eine geistige Bändigung der Form," "Selbstbeherrschung," and "eine 'kontemplative' Stimmung" (318), categories Rosenberg disdains to the same degree that Benn embraces them. For Rosenberg, every act of creation presupposes the forming will of the artist. Traditionally one has ignored "die Tatsache . . . daß hinter jedem Kunstwerk, so wie hinter einem religiösen Bekenntnis eine Kraft steht . . . daß jeder Kunstschöpfung ein gestaltender Wille zugrunde liegt" (319). In addition, every good artwork sets as its goal "eine Tatgewalt der Seele zu wecken" (319). For Rosenberg—to cite the same idea in a different text—dynamism is both the origin and the purpose of art: "gerade die willenhafte Bewegtheit [ist] Ursprung der Kunst und *deshalb* auch Sinn des Endeffekts: in der Seele des Kunstempfängers" (emphasis in the original).[35]

Benn, in direct opposition to Rosenberg, favors stasis over Nordic dynamism not only in his view of the ideal artwork but in his aesthetics of production and reception as well. Moreover, he specifically alludes to the Greek and Asian roots of *Statik*.[36] Viewed as implied opposition to Rosenberg's theories, Benn's seemingly pure poetry of stasis becomes a poetry of engagement and so offers an interesting—if (as I will suggest below) nonetheless not entirely adequate—answer to the central tension of modern poetry, the tension between formal autonomy and political purpose.[37] It is of course ironic that a figure banned from publishing partly because of his efforts to reconcile expressionism and national socialism should find his strongest anti-Nazi voice in a variant of classicism, in "schöpferische Bändigung" (*DD*, 92). In his panegyric of Julius Evola's *Erhebung wider die moderne Welt*, a book that assails modernity and elevates "die Traditionswelt," Benn writes: "Es gibt zwei Ordnungen, eine geistige und eine naturhafte: der Geist, das ist die Askese und die Form; die Natur, das ist der Mangel an Begrenzung" (*GW*, 4:256). For what abides, Benn turns not to nature or the experimental avant-garde, not to frenzy or future prophecy, but to classical form: "Was objektiv bleibt, ist nicht die Prophetie von Zukünften, sondern es sind die abgeschlossenen hinterlassungsfähigen Gebilde. Was bleibt, ist das zu Bildern verarbeitete Sein. Der Erfolg der Dynamik: Klassik! Hier halten wir, es ist 1940" (*GW*, 1:298). Throughout his earlier national socialist essays Benn had spoken approvingly of "die Bewegung";[38] in his embrace of classical form, and of stasis in particular, a counterposition is evident, the details of which are discernible only against the backdrop of Rosenberg's theories. Considering the numerous studies on Benn, it is remarkable that a book which sold over one million copies by 1943, the second bible of national socialism, has previously been overlooked in discussions of *Statik*.

Benn's embrace of stasis, as much as it derives from his encounter with Rosenberg, transcends Rosenberg and can be viewed as a counterposition to national socialist art as such.[39] One thinks first and foremost of national socialist poetry, which heralded the historical march into the future, elevated heroic and frenzied action, and celebrated *Führer* and *Volk*.[40] Benn's poetry, in contrast, thematizes stillness instead of historical progress, idyllic withdrawal instead of heroic action, cerebral indifference instead of storm and destiny, and the isolated individual instead of the collective. Benn's increasing distance from national socialism can be measured in part by his receding antiintellectualism. Rather than immersing himself in frenzy, he withdraws into his own self and coldly observes. In place of *Lebensraum*

Statik *and* Inner Emigration   49

and the breaking of frontiers, he calls for a wall around the self. National socialist poetry is, on the whole, communal poetry: first, it promotes collective participation and a common fate, as, for example, in Baldur von Schirach's "Gemeinschaft: Das Lied der Getreuen"[41] or Heinrich Anacker's "Auch du, auch du mußt mit" (71); second, it is designed for the group activities of singing and marching. The second national anthem of Nazi Germany, the "Horst Wessel Lied," is a good example: it is a song for and about marching, a march into an idealized future. The second and third stanzas read:

> Die Straße frei den braunen Bataillonen!
> Die Straße frei dem Sturmabteilungsmann!
> Es schaun aufs Hakenkreuz voll Hoffnung schon Millionen,
> der Tag der Freiheit und für Brot bricht an.
>
> Zum letzten Mal wird zum Appell geblasen,
> zum Kampfe stehn wir alle schon bereit.
> Bald flattern Hitlerfahnen über allen Straßen,
> die Knechtschaft dauert nur noch kurze Zeit.[42]

The recipient of the national socialist marching song, which contemporary literary historians referred to by the generic term "das Lied der Bewegung,"[43] is invited to become part of a historical progression. The recipient of Benn's poetry, on the other hand, is encouraged to ignore or transcend history. Benn's reader is ideally passive, not active. The instrumentality of art is replaced by an assertion of artistic autonomy. Where the National Socialists stressed youth,[44] the wise man of Benn's "Statische Gedichte" is oblivious to the emergence and claims of new generations. The Nazis employ stereotypical images, phrases, and metaphors; Benn, on the other hand, coins new phrases and presents elliptical allusions. A linear and heroic style gives way to an elusive, intellectual style that demands nonlinear rereading. A poetry aligned with the linearity and temporality of music is countered by a poetry more akin to the negation of time traditionally associated with sculpture.

The national socialist elevation of the communal and of linear marching is not restricted to poetry. Benn's circular recollection of what abides can also be seen in contrast to other national socialist artworks. A good example would be Hans Steinhoff's popular national socialist film *Hitlerjunge Quex* (1933).[45] This film, based on a novel by Karl Schenzinger, is a story of the German nation's choice, concretized in the figure of Heini Völker, between communism and nazism. The Communists are criticized not only for their actions and thoughts but also by way of their association with circular images: their sphere is that of the fair, with its merry-go-round, its lottery wheel, and the spinning targets of a shooting booth. This circularity represents directionlessness and dizziness, the lack of future vision. The associations are reinforced by the fact that the Communists are, on the whole, older individuals, while the Nazis are uniformly young. The one domestic scene among the National Socialists excludes the parents. In contrast to the circular imagery of the Communists, the National Socialists are associated with the linear motifs of marching and flag waving. Baldur von Schirach's "Unsre Fahne flattert uns voran," official song of the Hitler Youth and overture to this film, reveals the motifs of direction and purpose, of youth and the future, in the eightfold repetition of "Vorwärts!" in its first stanza and of "Jugend" in its second. The song's "heroic" refrain reads:

Unsre Fahne flattert uns voran,
in die Zukunft ziehn wir Mann für Mann.
Wir marschieren für Hitler durch Nacht und durch Not
mit der Fahne der Jugend für Freiheit und Brot.
Unsre Fahne flattert uns voran.
Unsre Fahne ist die neue Zeit.
Und die Fahne führt uns in die Ewigkeit!
Ja, die Fahne ist mehr als der Tod![46]

The eternal (the song's melody reaches its high point with the word "Ewigkeit") is not a timeless present but a sacrifice of the present for an unending progression in time.

Movement is also central to the most famous of national socialist films, Leni Riefenstahl's *Triumph des Willens*. The figures depicted in the film are generally in motion: one thinks of Hitler's entrance to Nuremberg, the morning activities of the rally participants, or the seemingly endless parade of marching soldiers. Moreover, when the subjects are not in motion, the camera is. The viewer has a sense of being caught up in the *Bewegung*. The Weimar mood of drift, of purposelessness, of ethical confusion is replaced by a sense of direction and purpose; one feels that one is part of historical destiny. An altogether different effect of the camera movement is the spectators' loss of orientation: with their eyes never at rest, they lose their grasp of the objective world. The film, through formal means, creates perspectival disorientation and a loss of objectivity. In an epistemological sense as well, Benn's embrace of *Statik* can be viewed as a counterposition to the *Bewegung* of national socialism.

While Benn's specific concept of stasis, as a counterstance to Rosenberg, appears to be a unique form of inner emigration, the elevation of form and clarity and the general embrace of stillness and stability as opposed to national socialist expediency and disorientation are common to a number of poets.[47] Fritz Diettrich, for example, addresses his own poetry as "still" and "abseits," as what brings "Klarheit" "in diesen Tagen, / Da alles schwankt":

> Du gibst uns in chaotischem Gedränge
> Die unbequeme Weisung, die uns frommt
> Und uns zuletzt versöhnt mit deiner Strenge.
>
> (1:358–59)

Friedrich Georg Jünger, in his oppositional poem "Der Mohn," first published in 1935, laments the feverishness and drunkenness that leads to sacrifices and casualties; in contrast, he elevates existential stillness and epistemological clarity:

> Schmerzend hallt in den Ohren der Lärm mir, mich widert der
>   Taumel,
> Widert das laute Geschrei, das sich Begeisterung nennt.
> Wehe! Begeisterung! Silberner Brunnen der Stille, du klarer,
> Du kristallener Born, nennt es Begeisterung nicht.
> Tiefer schweigen die Toten, sie trauern, sie hören das Lärmen,
> Hören das kindische Lied ruhmloser Trunkenheit nicht.
>
> (1:45)

Hans Leip takes a slightly different approach, heralding the stillness not of poetry but of the humble opponents of the present regime, those figures who are not seduced by power or rhetoric. He writes in 1942:

> Hab Achtung vor den Stillen,
> die im Lärmen
> der Menge
> unbeteiligt
> scheinen und ungerührt.
>
> (52)

Also akin to Benn's position is the stress on what abides and on what is inwardly attained. Rudolf Hagelstange writes in his *Venezianisches Credo* of 1945:

52 Statik *and Inner Emigration*

> Ihr müßt es wieder lernen, Euch zu trauen.
> Und Euer sicher sein, wo Sicherheit
> aus Tiefen kommt. Denn müßig ist der Streit
> um Wechselvolles. Und wir bauen
>
> Unsterbliches und Bleibendes hienieden
> nur aus dem geisterzeugten Stoff, dem nicht
> an Dauer, nicht an Herrlichkeit gebricht.
> Von ihm ist der vergängliche geschieden
>
> wie Ton von Marmor. Jener schafft Figuren,
> und mit Figuren füllt er seine Welt,
> die Welt der rasch verwehten Spuren,
>
> die sich dem Fluß der Zeiten zugesellt.
> Doch dieser wirkt aus trächtigen Basalten
> die Gegenwart unsterblicher Gestalten.
>
> (26)

Like Benn, Hagelstange contrasts the flux of temporality with a spirit able to transcend time and in this transcendence linked to the fixity of sculpture and the timelessness of art.[48]

The Rosenberg connection is again significant. In claiming legitimacy for his racial theories, Rosenberg denies the supremacy of reason and traditional philosophy's claims for universal truth.[49] For Rosenberg *Statik* signifies the transcendence of time and race. Benn, in his critique of Rosenberg and his affirmation of stasis, expresses a preference, not for history, but for the timeless; not the expedient, but the universal. Though Benn's poems are formally more interesting and stylistically more elusive than most writings by the authors of the inner emigration, the similar elevation of universality and stillness should not be overlooked.

The elevation of stillness is especially clear in Ernst Wiechert, a writer known first, perhaps, for taking the boldest public stand against national socialism of any poet who remained in Germany, and second, for writing sentimental, back-to-nature works that may seem to celebrate, as much as to undermine, national socialism. Wiechert's two university addresses—"Der Dichter und die Jugend" (1933) and "Der Dichter und seine Zeit" (1935)—are interesting not only as documents of his open resistance to the Third Reich but as reflections on the poet's relationship to what is still and eternal. In "Der Dichter und die Jugend" Wiechert writes of the poet, "daß er in einer lauten Welt der letzte und stille Bewahrer der ewigen Dinge ist" (10:361). He continues: "Sie sind die Bewahrer des Unvergänglichen und die stillen Mahner in einer lauten Welt. In allem Wandel der Zeiten und Meinungen ruht in ihrer Hand das Unwandelbare. In allem Verirrten und Angstvollen der Welt lösen und binden sie die Fäden der großen Ordnung, machen das Trübe klar, das Verwirrte einfach, das Schmerzliche heilig" (10:362). Wiechert heralds solitude and immersion in nature as catalysts to such reflection. He advises, "kehrt auch ein wenig zurück aus dem Lärm der Welt in die stillen Wälder," such that his listeners, like the poet, will learn *"das Stille zu bewahren"* (emphasis in the original, 10:367). In "Der Dichter und seine Zeit" Wiechert admonishes his contemporaries for being caught up in their own finite concerns and failing to recognize what is eternal. Here, too, the poet would lead the way: "unter allen lauten Worten und Liedern des Tages sucht er nach dem Stillen und Unvergänglichen" (10:371). In indicting the contemporary world's loss of clear values, Wiechert writes: "Ja, es kann wohl sein, daß ein Volk aufhört, Recht und Unrecht zu unterscheiden und daß jeder Kampf ein 'Recht' ist" (10:379). In the light of such crimes, tranquil reflection on eternal truth is, he concludes, not to be mistaken for simple silence (10:380).

The thoughts in these two famous addresses can be found developed and refined throughout Wiechert's writings. In *Jahre und Zeiten* he counters "das Vergängliche der Zeit" and sees himself, the poet, as "ein Sohn der Zeitlosigkeit" (9:702, 773). He suggests that one find the inner strength to counter "Meinung oder Geschrei der Zeit," including nationalism and aggression, by such acts as withdrawing into nature or history, or reading authors like Goethe and Stifter (9:702–3). In the short, programmatically Christian essay "Laut und Leise" Wiechert associates Christianity and salvation with stillness, while suggesting that the contemporary world, concerned with material progress and technological advancement, has turned its soul over to meaningless noise:[50]

> Laut und leise. Das sind die Pole der Zeit. Und es ist, als schwanke die Achse des Lebens langsam auf und nieder zwischen ihnen. Da sind laute Jahrhunderte und laute Jahre und laute Stunden, und es will uns manchmal scheinen, als bäume in ihnen und in ihnen allein die Woge des Lebens sich auf und umfasse allen Glanz unseres Daseins. Und wir vergessen, wie still das Große ist: Der Baum, der wächst, die Blume, die sich erschließt, das Tier, das aus abendlichen Wäldern tritt, das Gedicht, das aus dem Schweigen steigt, der Tod, der über eine Stirne fällt. (10:610–11)

"Die Stillen" are able to see clearly, to recognize when mankind has taken off in a false direction (10:611). Associating himself with the same tradition as does Benn, Wiechert suggests that it is "die Stillen . . . denen Gott im Schweigen erscheint" (10:609). A review of Wiechert's poems, works such as "Nur wer allein ist" (10:529-30) or "Abseits" (10:535-36), reinforces this image of a poet who embraces solitude and idyllic immersion in nature as the proper conditions for reflection on stillness and eternity. Wiechert's numerous novellas and novels only substantiate this claim.[51]

The differences between Benn and Wiechert are of course enormous and readily visible to anyone who has read both authors. Benn's poetry carries with it not a trace of the sentimentality that pervades Wiechert's; the alleged timelessness of Wiechert's art does not originate, as does Benn's, from an elevation of form; Wiechert's moral critique of fascism cannot be confused with Benn's conscious avoidance of the categories of content and morality; and finally, Benn's poetry differs from Wiechert's and virtually all other opposition poetry in its avoidance of any overtly didactic element. These and other differences, however, do not overshadow a moment shared by both authors, as well as by others writing during this era: the attempt to negate national socialism in part by pointing to a transcendence characterized by timelessness and stillness.

There is another dimension at play here: stasis, and the corollary negation of travel, as a justification for nonemigration.[52] Charles Hoffmann has cogently argued that "inner emigration" is a biographical rather than a literary concept;[53] yet in Benn's case one can use the biographical to help explain the literary, and vice versa. Stillness has a biographical or existential function: this is clear from "Reisen" and, to a lesser extent, from "Statische Gedichte" as well. Whatever comfort or salvation may be available amidst the chaos of modernity, and of the Third Reich in particular, is to be found in withdrawal and in poetry—specifically, poetic form and closure.[54] For Benn, the embrace of a static, self-enclosed aesthetic sphere derives more from existential disorientation and the desire for stability than from a programmatic philosophy of l'art pour l'art.[55] The absolute poem, as much as it purports to be autonomous vis à vis the world, fulfills a function for the poet's own attempts at centeredness. Benn mocks the wanderer and traveler, who feels the need to search elsewhere for the self. The emigrant, according to Benn, lacks stability and the strength to endure.[56] Rather than leaving Germany, Benn remained and employed poetry as a medium through which to sublimate his suffering and to survive under even the most chaotic circumstances. As in the tradition, art and *Ruhe* act as a kind of therapy—in Benn's own words, "ein katharisches Phänomen" (*GW*, 1:561)—though for him the therapy is individual, not universal.[57] For Benn, the external is secondary: this frees him to live his double existence under the most difficult conditions; however, it also gives him no reason to protest a nation that is itself on a destructive path. To the degree that the poet or sage is impervious to progress, he is also impervious to injustice.

One can, by way of external reflection, criticize the inner emigrants for not analyzing social and political structures, but one cannot criticize them for reflecting on structures of transcendence.[58] The two areas of inquiry—historical analyses and normative reflections—do not, in principle, exclude one another; on the contrary, they are mutually reinforcing.[59] One can analyze the inadequacies of the present only against an ideal other, even if this other remains merely implicit. What is timeless, meanwhile, becomes meaningful only insofar as it relates to what is finite and present.[60] Benn's unfortunate reduction of stasis to what is merely transcendent, merely formal, need not color the validity of his insight into the need for transcendence or his valid recognition, late as it was, of the untenability of history and experience as exclusive grounds of legitimacy.

7. National Socialism and Transcendental Norms

In his essay "Nach dem Nihilismus" Benn speaks of "die Auflösung aller alten Bindungen, die Zerstörung der Substanz, die Nivellierung aller Werte" (*GW*, 1:156). This loss of absolute norms was diagnosed not only by Benn but by a large number of intellectual figures of various persuasions—Robert Musil, Hermann Broch, Helmuth Plessner, Georg Lukács, Eugen Güster, to name only a handful. Though the causes were not always studied in detail—social, economic, and political factors generally received less attention than intellectual ones[1]—the diagnosis of a loss of traditional or transcendent positions was widespread[2] and, it seems, accurate.

Hermann Broch coined the phrase *Zerfall der Werte* and meant thereby the loss of a coherent, systematic world view, from which all individual positions derive.[3] Twentieth-century society has lost transcendent standards on which to base moral and political decisions and has replaced universal norms with partial value systems. The result is the absolutization of the relative in the form of such phrases as "war is war," "business is business," "art for art's sake," or, in the historically most devastating partial value system of all, the identification of the absolute with the nation-state, with Germany, rather than with the universal—the subordination, therefore, of universal norms to nationalist laws and duties. In order to substantiate my claim that the loss of an absolute world view contributed to the emergence of national socialism (and the corollary stance that Benn was justified in searching for an absolute perspective, even if his methods were inadequate), I offer here a brief critique of Nietzsche and Rosenberg. I argue that the national socialism of Rosenberg originated out of the Nietzschean affirmation of perspectivism and suspension of the law of noncontradiction—that is, Nietzsche's claim that an internal contradiction is no argument against a position. Benn's own affirmation of the regime in 1933 can also be viewed, at least in part, against this backdrop.

It is not my intention to enter the debate on whether Nietzsche was himself nationalist, imperialist, militarist, or anti-Semitic. (Walter Kaufmann has, I think, sufficiently disproved the picture of the proto-Nazi Nietzsche as it was promoted through the unethical editorial and exegetical work of Elisabeth Förster-Nietzsche and Alfred Bäumler.)[4] Rather, I would link Nietzsche with the historical possibility and logical necessity of power positivism, the view that truth is the privilege of the stronger—a position realized in the Third Reich.[5]

There can be no doubt that whatever Nietzsche's assertive stances may have been, his most fundamental claim—in the sense that it undermines all others—is that all positions are ultimately illusory, untenable, and ungrounded. Nietzsche insists on the impossibility of a first principle. All truth is perspectival, all knowledge is hypothetical, and all categories are historically conditioned. For Nietzsche there are no transcendent norms, "keine ewigen Horizonte und Perspektiven" (2:135). He writes: "Es gibt keine 'Wahrheit' " (3:497).[6] In a well-known passage the philosopher redefines truth as a form of error that serves life: "*Wahrheit ist die Art von Irrtum*, ohne welche eine bestimmte Art von lebendigen Wesen nicht leben könnte. Der Wert für das *Leben* entscheidet zuletzt" (emphasis in the original, 3:844). All evaluations are based on the preservation of a particular entity, be it an individual, a community, or a race (3:441). Values are measured by the strength and richness they give a particular valuing will. Nietzsche assumes the stance that the falseness of a judgment is no argument against it; indeed, false judgments that promote a particular life or species are to be privileged (2:569).[7] Contradictions are to be endured or embraced, not overcome (2:175).[8]

Nietzsche's perspectivism may appear at first glance to be liberating: because one's own truth is not final, one is free to listen to other positions, to develop "Tastorgane" for other perspectives (3:441).[9] This is a possible consequence, and it is surely the position of the mild Nietzsche and that of many attracted to the Nietzschean world view. One must ask, however, not what may be a contingent response to relativism, but rather what is its *logical* consequence.[10] A tolerance for other positions—without a transcendent measure by which to judge them—means that one has no valid argument against that position which itself denies tolerance. If no perspective is grounded, then why should I bother taking any perspective seriously other than my own? If there is no absolute, my own particular interests or those of another gain a stature they could not possibly have in a philosophy where the particular is subordinate to the universal. If universal standards of good and evil are abandoned, anything goes: "Nichts ist wahr, alles ist erlaubt" (2:889).[11] If everything is permitted, then so, too, is one individual's assertion of power over others. No legitimate *argument* can be made against those who assert the freedom to decide what is valid and what is invalid life.[12] Values, not being derived from a logical system, have no basis other than the arbitrariness of the individual will and the contingencies of the historical present.[13]

Nietzsche's personal notion of will to power may have little to do with the concepts of power and injustice developed by Thrasymachus and Callicles in Plato's dialogues *Republic I* and *Gorgias*, but that—even if it is true[14]—is not enough to counter the fact that power positivism is the ultimate consequence of Nietzschean perspectivism. Relativism cannot argue against power positivism; indeed, it passes over into it. This transition is not unrelated to Nietzsche's own view of the shift from passive nihilism (there is no truth, everything is equal) to active nihilism (there is no truth, therefore I am free to assert my position at the expense of others).[15] Because the values of the power positivist do not stem from any rational principles, they become whatever serves the power of the individual or group: secondary virtues such as discipline or sacrifice. Whatever goals these secondary virtues themselves serve remain ungrounded, and since reason has been abandoned—it makes universal claims that are untenable—it is not surprising that the power positivist turns to nature, blood, instinct, and race. The question of highest values becomes a purely decisionistic matter, one in which reason gives way to nature.

Both relativism and power positivism are philosophically untenable.[16] The statement "there is no truth" involves a pragmatic contradiction,[17] a contradiction between its content and its form, between the statement made and what is presupposed in the act of making the statement.[18] The proposition claims ahistorical truth even as it denies such truth.[19] One cannot, without refuting oneself, assert as true the claim that nothing is true. Since Nietzsche's own measure of evaluation is itself without foundation and since it can be asserted only insofar as one abandons the law of noncontradiction, philosophy becomes for Nietzsche not a matter of reason and rational debate but one of likes and dislikes. Injustice, or the prerogative of the powerful, becomes a principle of justice. One is free to choose and implement whatever position advances one's own power.

Power positivism, however, like relativism, cancels itself.[20] First, injustice always presupposes justice. For any number of individuals to get the strength to be unjust they must act justly by one another. The thought is not new to literary critics familiar with the real or expected loyalty within the robber bands of Schiller's *Die Räuber* (act I, scene 2) or Brecht's *Die Dreigroschenoper*, or with the legalistic mentality of Goethe's Mephistopheles (*Faust*, 1410–17). Taken on its own terms, injustice becomes an enemy not only to justice but to itself. Second, the unjust individual cannot attempt to convince others of the validity of his or her position in dialogue form without falling into a contradiction between the eristic theory of injustice and the conditions of discourse: fairness, consistency, and communicability. Dialogue is possible only within a framework of justice; it is therefore impossible to make a case for injustice without assuming the position one would deny. Insofar as the unjust individual remains a partner in dialogue, the victory of justice is decided a priori. Third, after denying the possibility of objective discourse to the unjust individual, it might be thought that such an individual could try to persuade others rhetorically and irrationally of the virtues of injustice, avoiding any direct confrontation with the arguments or structures of justice—but here, too, the unjust one would only lose the power that forms the core of the injustice. Insofar as unjust individuals encourage belief in the validity of injustice, they justify the violation of their rights by others. The unjust individual, therefore, "who attempts injustice rightly must be supposed to escape detection" and must support—theoretically at least—the idea of justice, under whose shield it is possible to remain unjust only by seeming to be just.[21] In short, to defend injustice is to place the unjust individual and injustice itself in danger. Unjust individuals not only presuppose what they would deny, they cannot make a case for injustice without canceling their own position. Relativism and power positivism are philosophically untenable because they contradict the conditions of their own truth; in short, they are self-canceling.[22]

One does not refute a position philosophically by drawing attention to its historical consequences;[23] nevertheless, an understanding of the historical, not merely the logical, proximity of Nietzschean perspectivism and national socialism is enlightening. Though national socialism is often viewed as a closed or absolute system, it must be recognized as an *arbitrary* absolute and therefore one that arises not from an absolute philosophy (there are universal truths) but from a relativistic position that has passed over into power positivism (because there are no universal truths, one subject or group of subjects has the right to assert its irrational truths over others). If one relativizes the absolute, one is free to absolutize the relative—and that, not absolute philosophy, is what national socialism was: an absolutization of the relative, namely power and race, as a result of the undermining of the absolute.[24]

This is clearly demonstrated in Rosenberg's highly successful *Mythus des 20. Jahrhunderts*.[25] Here, along with his elevation of dynamism over stasis, Rosenberg rebukes those systematic philosophers who assert the viability of a priori or absolute truths and who base values on logic and the law of noncontradiction.[26] He denies the existence of absolute norms or values: there are "keine absoluten Werte" (22); moreover, if there were any absolute values or eternal truths, it would be impossible for us to grasp them (681). He discredits "blutleere Werte, die das Naturvolle übersehen" (23). All positions are determined by historical conditions: "*Es gibt keine voraussetzungslose Wissenschaft, sondern nur Wissenschaft mit Voraussetzungen*" (emphasis in the original, 119). Rosenberg criticizes the philosophical search for absolute truth: "Gleich der hoffnungsvollen Antike sind auch alle heutigen Zunftphilosophen, im Ernst und aus Geschäft, auf der Suche oder auf der Jagd nach der sogenannten einen, ewigen Wahrheit. Diese Wahrheit suchen sie auf rein logischem Wege, indem sie von Axiomen des Verstandes weiter und weiter schließen" (681–82). Any philosophy that teaches logically deduced transcendent values errs (127). Values are to be created by the individual race or will; they cannot be discovered, nor can they be refuted, by logical analysis. Socrates, who spoke of "'das Gute' an sich" and claimed that virtue was universal, destroyed Greek culture (285); in recognizing only individuals and universals, he failed to understand the significance of race (286).[27] Even German philosophers have been prone to this mistake; Hegel's well-grounded assertion, "die Logik ist die Wissenschaft von Gott,"[28] is for Rosenberg "ein Faustschlag ins Gesicht einer jeden echten nordischen Religion, einer jeden echten germanischen . . . Wissenschaft" (287). Believing that logic is no criterion for truth, Rosenberg admonishes "den nur logischen Wahrheitssucher" (692).

Any claim to universal truth is, in Rosenberg's view, invariably false and dogmatic (125). He opposes knowledge of race to all universal philosophies: "Diese Erkenntnis . . . setzt uns . . . in schärfsten Gegensatz zu allen 'absoluten' 'universalistischen' Systemen, die von einer angeblichen Menschheit aus erneut auf eine Unitarisierung aller Seelen für alle Zukunft hinaus wollen" (136). Rosenberg contrasts empty, universal, logical truth with the organic truths of blood and race: "Damit ist jedoch auch schon eine ganz andere Auffassung von der 'Wahrheit' angedeutet: daß für uns Wahrheit kein *logisches* Richtig und Falsch bedeutet, sondern daß eine *organische* Antwort gefordert wird auf die Frage: fruchtbar oder unfruchtbar, eigengesetzlich oder unfrei?" (emphasis in the original, 690). In another passage he asserts: "Das ist der andere—'wahrere'—Strom des echt wuchshaften (organischen) Wahrheitssuchens entgegen dem scholastisch = logisch = mechanischen Ringen nach 'absoluter Erkenntnis'" (691). Humanity, dissolved of racial origins and considerations, is a meaningless fiction

(22), yet one that must be countered insofar as the concept of humanity dissolves racial identities and leads to valuelessness, "rasselose Wertelosigkeit" (120). Rosenberg's fear of this raceless universality is softened by his claim that there is really no communication among races.[29] He likens race to Leibniz's monads: "jedoch wird die Monade einer Persönlichkeit ganz fremden Blutes gegenüber erneut 'fensterlos' " (694). Having abandoned universal, coherent, and positive categories, Rosenberg absolutizes the negative figures of difference and otherness.

If values are not derived from reason, then surely from nature:[30] "Heute . . . beginnt ein ganzes Geschlecht zu ahnen, daß nur dort Werte geschaffen und erhalten werden, wo noch das Gesetz des Blutes Idee und Tat des Menschen bestimmt, sei es bewußt oder unbewußt" (22). Nature becomes a supreme value (140–42). In this respect Rosenberg and the Benn of 1933 have much in common. Though Benn was not anti-Semitic, he, too, believed in the failure of reason and so embraced a biological foundation for his view of not only historical motivation but also historical evaluation.[31] The thinker who abandons reason turns, quite consistently, to nature. For Nietzsche, the historical genesis of an idea proves its invalidity—that is, since all ideas are historically conditioned, all claims to ahistorical truth are invalid. Rosenberg draws the consequences of Nietzsche's position.[32] If all positions are historically conditioned, the better conditions must generate better truths: race usurps reason, history transcends philosophy.[33] Also Nietzschean in spirit is Rosenberg's assertion that ideas are determined by the body: "die 'Wissenschaft' ist eine Folge des Blutes" (120). Likewise based on perspectival philosophy is his justification for asserting that values should be affirmed in order to ennoble "das deutsche Volkstum . . . die Rasse zu kräftigen" (545). Because reason is no measure, the question Rosenberg asks is not 'Are the goals of the Nordic race legitimate?' but rather 'How can the Nordic race achieve power?'

Even if organic truth is erroneous, errors may still serve life (685–86)—and life is higher than reason, organic truth higher than the law of noncontradiction (683): "Dem Leben wird—abgesehen von allen Vernunftgesetzen—ein Eigenwert zugesprochen" (690). Rosenberg cites Nietzsche's argument: "nur das, was Leben schafft, hat Tugend, hat einen Wert" (691). It is in this spirit that Rosenberg can affirm any "truth" that serves the Germanic race: "im Dienste der organischen Wahrheit" means "im Dienst des rassegebundenen Volkstums" (684). Each culture, each race has its own "Höchstwert" (116), but if the highest value of one race calls for the elimination of another race, any protest is conditioned by the inferiority of the race that is to be eradicated. Without external restraints, the Germanic race has the right to assert its own superior path over others: "Heute verlangt diese echt organische Weltanschauung inmitten der zusammenbrechenden atomistischen Epoche mehr als früher: ihr Recht, ihr *Herrenrecht*" (emphasis in the original, 694–95).[34] The myth of blood must assert itself, and in doing so it need recognize no other highest values: "es fordert eine Weltrevolution und duldet keine anderen Höchstwerte mehr neben sich" (699). Because the highest values of other cultures restrict one's own, they must be eliminated (700). Rosenberg lays down the gauntlet against all who fail to recognize the supremacy of blood, specifically German blood: "die Ehre des deutschen Namens . . . kämpft gegen alle Mächte, die sie als ersten und höchsten Wert nicht gelten lassen wollen" (701). He is quite clear on the issue of might and right: both are subservient to *Volk*. As there are no universal standards for determining the good, justice is subordinate to the practical goals of race (571). "Recht . . . ist . . . für ewig an ein gewisses Blut geknüpft . . . mit dem es erscheint und mit dem es vergeht" (572). Since reason is not supreme, no argument against the Germanic world view is valid: "Der neue Mythus und die neue typenschaffende Kraft, die heute bei uns nach Ausdruck ringen, können überhaupt nicht 'widerlegt' werden" (700).[35]

The early twentieth-century failure to recognize and ground transcendent truths was not restricted to academic philosophy. A judicial corollary to perspectival morality and power positivism is the positive law theory of justice, a theory dominant in the Weimar era.[36] Moreover, the Weimar Constitution, as has been noted by thinkers as diverse as Carl Schmitt and Hermann Broch, lacked any absolute foundation.[37] It was a document dependent on legal positivism and a relativistic, consensus theory of truth. A two-thirds majority in parliament could change not just ordinary legislation but the most fundamental elements of the Constitution; thus, minorities were susceptible to majority rule. Still worse, a two-thirds majority could make arbitrary changes, and then conclude that the Constitution could never again be changed.[38] It was not merely Article 48 that gave Hitler a legal map to power; the Enabling Act of 24 March 1933, based on Article 76, guaranteed the lawful passage from Weimar to the Third Reich. A constitution without inalienable rights or absolute duties stems from a relativistic, rather than absolute, philosophy, and, as history has shown, such a constitution passes over into the tyranny of power positivism.[39] Either there are normative values that transcend democratic consensus, or it is illegitimate to protect, constitutionally, any position from shifts in consensus. Only a political structure based on logically coherent transcendent norms can guarantee individual rights when majority opinion opposes this or when historical changes occur.

An adequate solution to the problem of relativism and partial value systems could originate with the argument that there are transcendental structures on which the relativist depends even while denying them.[40] The best way to evaluate conflicting positions, perhaps the only way to allow for communication among them, is by immanent critique, the refutation of an alternative position on its own terms and on the basis of internal inconsistencies. If it can be shown that a proposition cannot be refuted without self-contradiction and without also necessarily presupposing the proposition to be refuted, then that proposition is necessarily true. Transcendental reflections of this kind represent the first step toward establishing a legitimate and coherent totality rather than the totalitarianism of an arbitrary standpoint.

One must clearly distinguish between those who make absolute claims blindly and irrationally and refuse to acknowledge the validity of immanent critique and those who arrive at their positions by exhibiting the self-cancellation of alternative positions.[41] Through the negation of untenable positions it is possible to apply a priori principles to shed light on complex political and judicial issues. In conjunction with the project of German idealism can be seen increased reflection on the philosophy of right, the creation of a coherent university system, the abolition of torture, arguments against the death penalty, and the development of new freedoms.[42] Within a Nietzschean framework, on the other hand, one cannot ground one's arguments against injustice; particular interests are no longer subordinate to transcendent truths, and justice is reduced to law or power. Early twentieth-century philosophers immersed in various forms of historicism and relativism did not recognize that their negation of all absolute principles gave irrational absolutists the *right* to assert whatever positions they desired.[43] Weimar was polarized intellectually by cultural and philosophical skeptics, ready to dismantle any hierarchy of intellectual positions, and extremists, who asserted the absolute rightness of their positions in such a way that they were incapable of considering alternatives. It is between the denial of absolute norms and the assertion of arbitrary absolutes that the technique of immanent critique, aided by the figure of self-cancellation, seeks to mediate.

Gottfried Benn did not map out an immanent critique of relativism; he did, however, present an intuitive affirmation of stasis, of that which transcends the contingencies of the present. It is Benn's strength to have recognized the need for that which partially transcends history and to have expressed this need so eloquently, but his weakness to have associated this transcendence with what is irrational, hermetic, and undialectical—a topic to be explored in the next chapter.

8. Critique

There is little doubt of the formal precision of the poems analyzed, the richness of their intellectual-historical allusions, or the importance of Benn for a study of the concept of stillness in twentieth-century Germany. What remains to be considered is the tenability of Benn's concept of stasis.[1] My critique will focus on three partly overlapping issues: first, the nonspecificity of Benn's position, which relates to his formalism and decisionism; second, the subjectivism of his poetry, which culminates in the self-contradictory concept of the monologue poem; and third, his cultivated indifference, which in effect supports positions that he nominally opposes. Nevertheless, Benn's concept of stasis is not without an element of truth.

Formalism

Under stasis can be understood those insights that are valid independent of changing historical circumstances. The content Benn gives to this transcendent moment, however, is purely formal and aesthetic; it has little to do with justice or goodness and is politically and ethically indeterminate. Stasis is merely the formal act of asserting an aesthetic construct: "Innerhalb des allgemeinen europäischen Nihilismus, innerhalb des Nihilismus aller Werte, erblicke ich keine andere Transcendenz als die Transcendenz der schöpferischen Lust" (*GW*, 4:235). The position by which Benn distances himself from national socialism does not in principle differ from the national socialist position itself: each negates the historical present for its chaos and lack of meaning; each appears justified by the fact alone that it promises a transcendence of this emptiness. There are of course countless and significant differences between Hitler's unjust, collective formalism and Benn's seemingly innocuous, asocial formalism, but they share two significant elements: formal appeal in a world of disorientation; and arbitrariness vis-à-vis content.[2] In late Weimar when there were competing parties, Benn actively worked for the freedom of the intellect; as soon as the National Socialists had an exclusive hold on power, he argued that all writers should serve the state.[3] National socialism received legitimacy by virtue of its position as the embodiment of totality. National socialist values appeared valid not because they were true, but because belief in them gave the individual a sense of order and stability.[4] Carrying a seed of truth (the need to pass beyond mere disorientation), Benn's elevation of stasis, not unlike national socialism itself,[5] remained decisionistic.[6] Interestingly, one of the intellectual fathers of national socialism,[7] Moeller van den Bruck, likewise embraced a concept of *Statik* (278) and, also like Benn, elevated the spatial over the temporal (238–39)—yet Moeller's stasis is identified neither with what is universal nor with what is unique, but rather with what is national and German. The contrast points to the dangers of a concept of stasis that is nebulously articulated and whose validity is based solely on experience or appeal.

It is not the moment of transcendence, itself a formal advance over chaos and relativism, that is the problem; rather, it is the lack of a measure by which to judge the validity of that transcendence. By affirming a merely formal alternative, Benn did not pass beyond his position of 1933, when his criticism of the critics of the Third Reich suggests there are in principle no valid standards by which to condemn the supposed injustice of the new state: "es gab niemals eine Qualität, die außerhalb des Historischen stand" (*GW*, 1:445). He dogmatically asserts the reduction of transcendence to history: "eine absolute Qualität gab es nie . . . Im Grunde hat immer nur die Geschichte gedacht" (*GW*, 1:445). For an author—the Benn of 1933—who argues that the legitimacy of a position is its historical development, norms can play no significant role. Nor can they play a significant role for an author—the Benn of the 1940s—who views form as the only possible transcendence.

In his static poems Benn calls on us—much as does Heidegger in *Sein und Zeit*—to experience the stillness of our own selves.[8] Heidegger's famous call of conscience is characterized by *Schweigen*: "Dem angerufenen Selbst wird 'nichts' zu-gerufen, sondern es ist *aufgerufen* zu ihm selbst, das heißt zu seinem eigensten Seinkönnen" (273). But this call of conscience, much like Benn's plea for a stable self in the poem "Reisen," is purely formal, empty of ethical guidelines. Benn's absolute, like Heidegger's, is devoid of specific content. One is reminded of the anecdote that a student of Heidegger's once exclaimed "ich bin unheimlich entschlossen—ich weiß nur noch nicht, wozu!" Benn goes so far as to celebrate this elimination of content; it allows him to escape the dynamism of Heideggerian *Entschlossenheit* and reassert stasis. Though it is important that ethical relativism and injustice be met with a stable (or static) position, it is equally important that the position be grounded. The merely formal affirmation of a position can be shared by the power positivist and the aesthetic poet. In *Tri-*

umph des Willens Hitler calls his movement "einen ruhenden Pol [in der] Flut der Erscheinungen," echoing a Heraclitean rhetoric that is also the basis of Benn's "Wer allein ist—."[9]

If we recognize, with Benn, "eine Absolutheit des Formalen" (*GW*, 1:213), then any political position can be aestheticized and made beautiful. Benn's national socialism cannot be reduced to the mistaken belief that art would be autonomous under the Nazis—though this is a significant element; his infatuation with the movement relates as well to their aestheticization of politics.[10] If form is the only significant criterion, there is no compelling reason not to affirm the National Socialists' attractive displays of power and transcendence of chaos.[11] Benn's submission to national socialism's aestheticized politics is from this perspective not surprising. Fascist propaganda envelops itself in a rhythmic, almost hypnotic, frame: marches, flags, uniforms, daily rituals, celebrations, and so forth. The efficacy of Hitler's speeches appears to derive from tone, gesture, emphasis—from form more than from content.[12] The magical force of such rhetoric is not unlike that of a merely formal poetry.[13] The viewer, not grasping any clear content, is nonetheless unable to resist its allure. Writing in 1949, Benn still held to the supremacy of form over substance: "Stil ist der Wahrheit überlegen, er trägt in sich den Beweis der Existenz" (*GW*, 4:159). According to the same logic, the historical atrocities of national socialism are superior to whatever normative theories might have helped us avoid such atrocities.

One can of course stress the differences between Benn and national socialism, as I did in an earlier chapter, but such an approach, by itself, would be misleading. In his provocative article "NS-Literatur und Modernität," Uwe-K. Ketelsen raises the question whether national socialism and modernism might not share certain common features. Discussing national socialist drama, for example, Ketelsen notes a basic, recurring structure whereby the hero, through an act of pure will, creates meaning in a situation viewed as meaningless or absurd. The thrust behind the hero's development is a purely decisionistic one: what is important is not the content but the simple affirmation of meaning, the will to live despite the chaos of the world. Ketelsen notes that this structure also pervades much of modern literature. The situation, one could argue, is the legacy of Nietzschean relativism and Heideggerian *Entschlossenheit*, which operate with the concepts of perspectival disorientation and decisionistic resolve. That perspectivism and decisionism have catalysts in the widespread economic, political, and social ruptures of the early twentieth century reinforces the suspicion that the issue has more than merely intellectual roots and is not unique to Benn, to national socialism, or even to Germany.

It is in this context as well that one might consider the formalism prominent among writers attempting to cope with the upheavals of twentieth-century Germany. Theodore Ziolkowski has argued in "Form und Protest" that writers of the inner emigration viewed the historical present as a time of chaos to which they countered the formal stillness, symmetrical order, and traditionalism of the sonnet. What one finds in Benn's early embrace of national socialism (the will to form, the dissolution of chaos, a new law) is what authors of the opposition saw in poetry. Rudolf Hagelstange writes, for example, concerning the sonnet: "In ihrer strengen Form . . . manifestierte sich schon äußerlich der Unwille gegen das Formlose, der Wille zu neuem Gesetz . . . das Sonett, gegen den Ungeist kreiert, wurde geradezu zu einer Modeform des Widerstandes" ("Die Form," 36). Through poetry, which is, according to Hagelstange, itself timeless, one can overcome temporal chaos. The theme of his sonnets, he writes, is "die Überwindung des zeitlichen Chaos durch Besinnung auf über= und außerzeitliche Kräfte des Menschen" (36).[14] Cornelia Jungrichter has shown, in response to Ziolkowski, that the sonnet form was used for the transmission of Nazi as well as anti-Nazi content.[15] While her claim does not diminish the correctness of Ziolkowski's analysis of the *intentions* of the oppositional poets, it does raise questions as to the sufficiency and validity of mere form as protest. Moreover, it reinforces Ketelsen's claim that formalism and decisionism are modern phenomena that envelop national socialism as well as much of avantgarde art. Adding to the data, one might note that the turn from Weimar to the Third Reich was viewed by many contemporaries as one from chaos to order.[16] In a tribute to Stefan George prepared during the period when he heralded national socialism, Benn himself addressed the proximity of aesthetic form to political order: "Sagen Sie für Form immer Zucht oder Ordnung oder Disziplin oder . . . Anordnungsnotwendigkeit, alle diese Worte, die uns so geläufig wurden, weil in ihrem Namen auch die geschichtliche Bewegung sich zu prägen versucht, das ist Georgesches Gebiet" (GW, 1:473).

Benn's formalism plays a role on the finite level of his poetic images as well. In "Statische Gedichte" Benn would counter Nietzsche's dynamic perspectivism with the more stable Renaissance notion of perspective.[17] But the concept and potential uses of perspective are as unstable as perspectivism itself. The artist who works with perspective may adopt a conventional technique and place in the foreground what is essential, letting what is insignificant recede, or may instead, following a religious tradition, create a work in which the background is highlighted: the painter draws a sacred path to the holy. Thus, in a broader sense, one's personal perspective still plays a role. Moreover, the illusionist potential of perspective must be considered: artists such as the fifteenth-century Paolo Uccello, the eighteenth-century Giovanni Piranesi, or the contemporary M. C. Escher employ perspective in order to trick viewers and undermine their orientation; this leads to a coupling of linear perspective and perspectivism. Paintings that draw attention to their formal devices, to their own deception function, stress the distinction between three-dimensional and two-dimensional art. While sculpture has a certain independence, painting depends on a viewer; indeed, painting depends on the deception of the viewer (the canvas *is* two-dimensional) even as it purports to capture reality. The formal stress within painting that leads to this self-reflexive perspectivism would seem to mirror Benn's own stress on formalism in the realm of poetry. Hegel's description of the subordination of content to form in painting, "die subjektive Kunst des Machens [wird] zur Hauptsache" (15:35), applies to Benn within the sphere of poetry: what is arbitrary and contingent, the poet's subjective affirmation of form, is eternalized at the expense of substance.[18] Benn's attempt to counter Nietzsche by way of the formal structure of perspective is misguided; the truth of perspective is perspectivism.

Beyond the issue of pure formalism as it relates to twentieth-century art and national socialist politics is the distinct, but related, issue of Benn's inability to counter national socialism in a philosophically coherent manner. In "Statische Gedichte" he suggests that since all positions are illusory, to take any position is to err. The only valid position is one of indifference. But because indifference is itself just another illusory position, an equally legitimate stance would be the active nihilism of destruction. With his formalist position Benn cannot *argue* against the power positivism of national socialism. Moreover, viewed on a metalevel, Benn's indifference is the reverse side of power positivism: it is the result of his longing for independence. Power positivism would claim its independence from existing reality by actively and arbitrarily negating its institutions. Like the Cynics of the Greek and Roman worlds, with whom Benn has much in common, the poet can only watch as his political "partners" destroy a world whose validity he would agree is, after all, only relative.

As I suggested earlier, Benn was engaged with problems resulting from the contemporary world's loss of an absolute value system.[19] His poetry represents the search for an aesthetic absolute that would overcome nihilism and assume the role left vacant by the loss of religious faith and philosophical truth. Artists represent for Benn "die letzten Reste eines Menschen, der noch an das Absolute glaubt und in ihm lebt" (GW, 1:520). The poet places "gegen den allgemeinen Nihilismus der Werte eine neue Transzendenz" (GW, 1:500). Benn's effort to found the absolute in the stillness of art may be mistaken in a sense that transcends the problems of his own formalism: if nihilism is the inability to ground values, then it is difficult to see how art can overcome nihilism. Art can provide us with insights into the consequences of nihilism; it can also provide a temporary and illusory, if also proleptic, stilling of its effects. Moreover, art can dramatize the need for truth and suggest directions for seeking it. But art cannot, without itself becoming philosophy, ground values, or justify the claim that it can ground values. In fact, without becoming philosophy, art cannot even legitimate its own existence. What is needed in the wake of the political and ethical consequences of decisionism is not aestheticism, but the rehabilitation of transcendental arguments, which alone can ground a priori norms.[20] One cannot demand that a poet provide us with ethical norms, but one can criticize—from an ethical standpoint—a poet who views aesthetics as the only valid location of norms. One cannot criticize an author for finding comfort in aestheticism, yet one can criticize an author who views aestheticism as the only answer to contemporary ills and terrors and so works against the possibility of any substantive content or of the unity of form and content.[21]

Subjectivism

One of the most central issues since the breakdown of German idealism is intersubjectivity, the concern not with subject-object but with subject-subject relations. Benn's poems tend to ignore this aspect of postidealist philosophy and culture: their focus is not subject-subject relations, but the poet's grappling with objective being. The second stanza of "Wer allein ist—" with its mockery of intersubjective relations and its celebration of the artist's consciousness underlines this point. Moreover, the addressee of a Benn poem is frequently the mirror image of the poetic self, as, for example, in "Trunkene Flut" or "Statische Gedichte." The poems redound to assurances rather than dialectical structures or processes of reflection. In addition, they remain, in Benn's own words, essentially private, "monologisch" (GW, 1:547). The poem is not directed to its listeners as much as it revolves silently within itself. Consistent with the elevation of stasis, the poem is to have no effect. The denial of a recipient seems to guarantee this structure. Benn himself speaks of "das Gedicht an niemanden gerichtet" (GW, 1:524). Much of what the poet would claim to know must remain a mystery, and so it is no surprise that in a recent dissertation Regina Weber suggests that Benn owes a great deal to the tradition of gnosticism.[22] Though Benn may justly assert that contemporary discourse is overwhelmingly shallow,[23] his private and hermetic mysticism, which even in his own eyes should pass over into silence,[24] hardly answers this problem.[25] Not only does one recognize here a counterproductive hermeticism, Benn's elevation of the self frees him from engaging other views and shades him from political and social context.[26]

The subjectivism of the poet and the apparent substantiality of what abides collapse into one. The denial of content even in the service of objectivity reinforces, behind its own back, the subjective impulse. Because it is not possible to determine the good or the just, the poet surreptitiously enjoys the status of being identical with the highest position available to humankind, and does so without having to consider alternatives or argue for the validity of such a stance. There is a striking similarity not only between the formalism of national socialism and Benn's view of poetry, but also between his monologue poetry and his earlier view of national socialism as "monistisch, antidialektisch" (GW, 1:214). The other, which Benn cannot define but can only circumscribe ("hinüberlangen in jenes andere—in was?"),[27] is so vague and empty as to be a merely subjective projection.[28] Benn's loyalty to objective truth and his unwillingness to define this truth are one with his subjectivism.

Benn's claim to be able to draw ethical consequences from art ("eine neue *ethische* Realität" [GW, 4:161]) deviates from a view of ethics as knowledge of the good. For him, aesthetic creation usurps traditional ethics: "alle ethischen Kategorien münden für den Dichter in die Kategorie der individuellen Vollendung" (GW, 4:221). The poet's affirmation of stasis as an ethical category remains locked within a private ethics and is as such the negation of ethics. Moreover, if art has no purpose (and ideally no effect), the ethics of art becomes an ethics of indifference, indeed an ethics that would cancel itself as soon as it made a plea on its own behalf. "Statische Gedichte" is in part a victim of this problem. The contradiction in Benn's attempt to communicate the truth of isolated subjectivity illustrates, in a performative rather than propositional manner, that subjectivity is after all not the highest truth.[29] Our knowledge of Benn's monologic efforts presupposes a dialogic sphere of explication.[30]

Indifference

Having briefly discussed the formalism and subjectivism of Benn's poetry, I turn now to his revisions of the tradition and the consequences of these revisions for politics. Benn employs the language of mysticism in poems like "Trunkene Flut" or "Reisen" but empties his rhetoric of all religious content. Not only does he advocate an unhallowed mysticism, he, unlike the Middle and Late Stoics, abandons social responsibility and the sage's ideal of friendship. In his ninth letter Seneca explicitly criticizes the suggestion that the wise man attain tranquillity of mind by removing himself from all contact with the world; repose and service to society are reciprocally beneficial.[31] Seneca stresses, not withdrawal, but integration and friendship.[32] The Middle and Late Stoics argued that a proper peace of mind enables the self to act in harmony with society: *tranquillitas animi* leads to integration and responsibility, not isolation or insensitivity.[33] Not only does Benn deviate from the fullness of religious mysticism and the intersubjective ideals of Stoicism, his idealist leanings take idealism into a new arena. In a poem like "Wer allein ist—" he embraces the absolute sphere of idealist art. He seems to distinguish—as many of his contemporaries do not—between an instrumental, technical reason, which he mistrusts or even detests,[34] and a higher reason that represents the basic irrefutability of thought.[35] For the legitimacy of his claims, however, Benn can appeal, only irrationally, to his artistic mission, his selection as poet and seer. His assertions are not grounded in anything beyond his own subjectivity and isolation ("Wer allein ist, ist auch im Geheimnis") or his self-proclaimed tragic suffering, and these are hardly valid criteria for aesthetic truth. Undifferentiated unity, the unconscious, even suffering are prominent in idealist aesthetics, but they are normally superseded by self-reflection and attempts at legitimation that bring art into the sphere of philosophy—as, for example, in the work of Hölderlin.[36] Benn's elevation of thought, on the other hand, falls back into a kind of dogmatism; its validity derives not from the consistency and immanence of its claims, but rather from its origins and rhetoric alone.

In the sphere of politics Benn's position is equally problematic. The origins of his embrace of *Statik*, as the comparison with Rosenberg showed, are clearly political; but a stasis that passes over into formalism and the negation of position-taking loses its political thrust and credibility. Though stasis, viewed as the negation of contemporary history, functions as a critical concept, when viewed in the light of the idea that history cannot or should not be changed, it has a fatalist dimension that renders its critical import impotent. Benn's reception reinforces this point. The poet's popularity after the war appears to have derived in part from his declaration of the futility of political action—including, of course, resistance—and his legitimation of passivity and neutral observation. The Benn of "Statische Gedichte," no different from the Benn of 1933, disparages the mundaneness of everyday, empirical politics and is unaffected by acts of injustice.

Resistance is not normally judged by virtue of external success, yet here a fundamental, not a contingent, error is at play. The elevation of stasis occurs less in conflict with the world than alongside it. Stasis is, as we have said, on the one hand, eternal truth—and with this, a standard by which one can resist the expedient instrumentalization of humanity; yet it is also stillness and withdrawal, and as such it represents the ineffectiveness of interiority. While it does not follow that reflection on ahistorical norms must lead to a turn away from reality (it could of course, and should, ultimately lead to a desire for the realization of these norms), it can be shown that writers of the inner emigration, among them Benn, did in fact often denigrate the importance of history in relation to the transcendent other. They proposed a totality that excluded history.[37]

Benn, wanting to assert independence above all, stresses, even more than his contemporaries, the difference between his sphere and the sphere of the world. However, in distancing himself from all ideologies or *Richtungen*, he effectively sides with the power of the majority. To counter the arbitrary totalitarianism of a single *Weltanschauung* by suggesting, as he does in "Statische Gedichte," that one embrace no *Weltanschauung*, is self-defeating. The "beautiful soul" that would not be tarnished by action is blemished by its refusal to act and thus by its support of ruling opinion.[38] Benn's separation of the private and the public, along with his elevation of the former, might be viewed as the culmination of a religious concept whose roots go back to Luther's reading of Romans 13 and his doctrine of two realms. Luther's positions are echoed in the passivity with which much of the German population met the conservative restoration of the nineteenth century and the instrumental authoritarianism of the twentieth.[39] The concept of two realms is directly apparent in the title of Benn's own *Doppelleben*. In becoming an acknowledged advocate of Luther's doctrine,[40] Benn fails to recognize that his stillness serves the purposes, not of negation and resistance, but of affirmation and consent.

Benn's sense, as a physician, that objective truth is restricted to the natural sciences appears to have led him to the claim, quite common in the modern world, that ethical positions are singularly subjective and the domain of the individual's personal interest.[41] In the face of this dissolving attitude, technical structures have become more and more universal, bringing the world to the brink of self-destruction; in such a world the need for universal, rather than private, values becomes ever more severe.[42] Benn's concept of stasis, however, remains subjective and restricted; it is an ideal of indifference and emptiness, not one of engagement. The synthesis of opposites that Benn invokes in his static poetry does not contain the particularity of life and so fails on its own terms. His ideology of aesthetic stillness cannot counter nihilism, and his quietism cannot stem political movements informed by unjust goals. His insight, however, into the need for stable and transcendent positions—what he calls *Statik*—should not be lost in an age of continuing crisis, nor should his rhetorically powerful and intellectually informed artistic invocations of this idea.

9. Theoretical Postscript

As mentioned in the Introduction, I call these readings "aesthetic" in derivation of a definition of art as the sensuous appearance of truth. Consequently, I have been attentive above all to two dimensions: first, the formal presentation of the poems, including the ways in which content is a function of form and vice versa; and second, the coherence and validity of the ideas expressed in the works. Further, in order to unravel the poems, I have found it necessary to focus on intellectual-historical allusions. An intellectual-historical moment is also present in my attempt to situate Benn's poems in the context of inner emigration as well as within the history of the idea of *Ruhe*.

The ill repute that intellectual history still suffers in the eyes of many literary critics stems, first, from the fact that often, rather than employing the intellectual-historical method to shed light on a literary work, scholars have pointed to texts as documentary proof of particular historical developments. Intellectual history often fails to account for the text as an aesthetic construct. To counteract this, I have traced the meanings of Benn's formulations from within the poems themselves, and only by way of the poems have I drawn attention to external factors. In pursuing the meanings of cryptic passages one does need to move beyond the poems. It is one of the critic's tasks to enrich the reader's understanding of a poem by unraveling allusions and in the process demonstrating how the poem uses traditional images or motifs in either new or traditional ways. Without a knowledge of Greek mythology, one cannot begin to grasp "Trunkene Flut." Without a knowledge of Greek philosophy or the German literary tradition, one remains blind to the rich dimensions of "Wer allein ist—." A knowledge of Aristotle, Seneca, and Meister Eckhart, to name only three pronounced influences, has the same function in our readings of "Statische Gedichte" and "Reisen." Our understanding of the intellectual-historical allusions in these poems has influenced our understanding of not only the content but also the formal structures of these works. Intellectual history, used as a tool of close reading, has become anything but an exercise in external criticism.

A second objection to the intellectual-historical focus stems from a more sociologically oriented reading process, which argues that artistic structures should be viewed first and foremost by way of their sociological genesis: texts are products of particular historical and class settings and corresponding ideological mind-sets. To this I would counter that literary works do have a genesis, but this is true only in the most trivial sense; all intellectual endeavors have a genesis. With this nothing is said about a work's literary or philosophical value. Historical conditions help us grasp what authors may have meant to say and why they said what they said or in what ways their positions are (or are not) representative of their times, but the focus on origins does not help us recognize whether what the author said is valid, that is, whether the ideas in the work are true. Historical conditions thus do little to help us evaluate the text's aesthetic worth. The aesthetic dimension, what one understands by the literary structures and the philosophical value of the work—which alone determine its universality or lack of universality—is reduced to a genealogical one. Benn's definitive embrace of static poetry is in part a development of his earlier metaphysical and historical cynicism, in part the consequence of his increasing elevation of form, in part an attempt to justify withdrawal in the face of national socialist calamities. It would be erroneous to declare that Benn's assertion of ahistorical truth is false because it developed as a result of these biographical and historical factors. Validity is not determined by genesis. One must distinguish between the external conditions—be they historical, psychological, technological, or whatever—that lead to the conception of an idea or the completion of a work, and the far more important conditions under which a statement can be true or false, its philosophical presuppositions.[1] To criticize Benn's particular ahistoricism one needs to do more than point to its genesis in a particular historical setting. In my critique of Benn, therefore, I have been primarily attentive not to the sphere of discovery but to the sphere of validity, the philosophical coherence of Benn's poetic statements.

My response to the sociologically oriented criticism of intellectual history thus brings me to my aesthetic orientation, and with it my stress on the coherence of the texts' ideas rather than on the conditions of their genesis.[2] In adopting this approach, I attempt to avoid a third and final problem with the intellectual-historical method: the frequent description of ideas in their intellectual-historical sequence without a philosophical analysis of their validity.

In focusing on philosophical coherence, I do not mean to deny that art has in part the function to sketch multivalent positions, to portray ambiguities. What is important is the level at which these ambiguities are portrayed and the extent to which they become linguistic corollaries of a more complex unity. Not all statements in a literary work aspire to universality, and there are many ambiguities that do not lead to overarching philosophical contradictions: for example, the identity of the *Schöpfergestalt* in "Trunkene Flut," our reading of the valley in "Statische Gedichte," or the connotations of *Grenze* in the poem "Reisen." Though we can make arguments in favor of one reading or another, these ambiguities are not completely resolved. The poem evokes in each case a multiplicity of possibilities, a multiplicity of meanings, and they must be read together—that is, within a higher, more complex unity.[3] The philosophical tenability of a text's statement does not rise or fall on the ambiguity of such finite passages. If, however, the statement of a literary work were that all positions are necessarily illusory, necessarily untenable, then the work's own claim that this is so, would be untenable—and so the work, in its claim, would cancel itself.[4] Such a work may be formally interesting but in the long run aesthetically weak. If a text deals with complex philosophical issues yet resolves them without itself becoming a contradictory work, then it has met, from a philosophical standpoint, a standard of excellence; the remaining task for the critic is to consider the value of the text's formal structures and emotional import. There are of course works that remain contradictory on the level of their general statements. The existence of ontological contradictions cannot be denied. To praise a work, however, precisely because it does *not* resolve contradictions would be to abandon the law of noncontradiction, without which all thought is arbitrary and all evaluation reduced to external conditions of power. Some texts tackle great and complex problems but fail to resolve them. Such works can be masterful, and their very nonresolution may give them a certain dramatic impetus; yet one should recognize that their excellence derives from the effort to push contradictions to their conclusion, not from the fact that they fail to resolve them. Much of Benn's writing belongs in this category: it is complex not only on the level of its finite images and allusions, but also on the general level of its wrestling with abstract philosophical issues.

The literature on Benn and politics tends to focus either on the historical details of Benn's brief declaration for national socialism or on the psychological and historical background that led him to find this movement attractive. Historical and genetic work along these lines is valuable in its own right; yet by itself it fails to illuminate the literary elements of Benn's poetic works, and it cannot evaluate his positions. Critics who would uncover the political deficiencies in Benn's artistic creations must be able to ground their positions or enter into an immanent critique—that is, accept Benn's position in order to demonstrate its internal inadequacies.

It is ironic that skepticism toward transcendental norms has resulted in a shift in literary criticism toward psychoanalytic, sociological, and historical studies, and that many of these studies purport to be rigorous in their critique of ideology, when in fact their very abandonment of absolute norms makes their critique, and the foundation of that critique, arbitrary. The problem of *Ideologiekritik* is one of enlightenment. Are the measures used to criticize other positions themselves grounded? If not, then the critique is ungrounded, and its claim to truth—that is, its claim for the falsity of alternative positions—itself ultimately ideological.

Even the critic who argues that he or she is merely uncovering an author's naive and mistaken belief in a priori norms, cannot, without adopting an absolute position, consider the author's position invalid. If one were to oppose Benn by asserting that ahistoricism is in principle false (all positions are conditioned, there are no absolute truths), then this very assertion must be conditioned and in principle false. Any global negation of ahistoricism is itself ahistorical and thus self-canceling.[5]

Evaluation is essential to the practice of literary criticism. Today there may seem little danger that informed critics will simply adopt the attitudes of the authors they are analyzing. Nonetheless, the figure by which authors become authorities for the private metaphysics of the critic occasionally recurs when the author becomes an authority on the dissolution of truth. The practice is a bit more subtle, but for that no less invalid. Because the author asserts that there is no truth—or that if there were any truth we couldn't know it—or that if there were truth, and we could know it, we still couldn't communicate it—the critic is unaware of having adopted a truth statement in siding with the author (whom the critic really shouldn't be able to understand, even if the author had something to say). Given, then, the need for evaluation, the need for critics to distance themselves from authors and weigh their positions, and the apparent lack of a grounded position from which this evaluation is to take place, immanent critique becomes an essential tool of the literary critic.

In the light of this situation, I have made an effort to sketch in my evaluation of Benn such positions as the following:

> An author who asserts that there are no absolute truths cannot even recognize the truth of this statement; such a position is contradictory, self-canceling, untenable.

> An external critique of the content of a position from a stance that does not ground itself is structurally similar, in its formalism and decisionism, to the position criticized.

An embrace of stillness and stasis whose legitimacy derives merely from experience is philosophically no different from the elevation of a position insofar as it is based on nature.

An elevation of form at the expense of content leaves one with no compelling reason not to accept an aestheticization of politics engineered with unjust goals in mind.

A monologic art is a contradiction in terms. Not only can one not argue for this position without contradicting oneself, the truth of such art is silence.

The artist who embraces withdrawal in order to be free of the political sphere remains within the political sphere insofar as the lack of voice becomes implicit consent for the ruling opinion.

A true absolute is not exclusive and so contains within it a concern for the realization of norms in history.

10. Summary

This study opened with an analysis of "Trunkene Flut," a Dionysian work in which only by reading against the grain could we recognize the poem's hidden Apollinian moments, closure and stillness. Next to be considered was "Wer allein ist—," one of Benn's most famous affirmations of aesthetic stillness. Varying a series of motifs that reach back to the pre-Socratics, Benn views stillness as the essence of absolute art. In "Statische Gedichte" he associates the poet with the sage: only a person who avoids distractions and exhibits ἀταραξία and αὐτάρχεια can find true peace of mind. Stillness is also an epistemological ideal. Benn's perspectivism, unlike Nietzsche's, suggests that only from a position of stability or stasis can one recognize the inadequacies of everyday disorientation and envisage the absolute. In "Reisen" Benn allies himself with specific aspects of the mystic and Stoic traditions, even as he deviates from their most hallowed religious and intersubjective ideals. The expansive Dionysian transcendence of "Trunkene Flut" becomes in this later work a tranquil, self-enclosed transcendence.

The four spheres in which *Ruhe* has traditionally played a role—religion, aesthetics, psychology, and politics—are all evident in Benn. In a religious context Benn alludes to the Aristotelian elevation of motionlessness and the Christian veneration of repose; in each case, however, he alters the specifically religious moment. The poet assumes the role of Aristotle's unmoved mover and usurps Christ both as the model sufferer and as the figure whose quietude and repose are exemplary for humanity. Abandoning an earlier commitment to dynamism and dissonance, Benn adopts an aesthetic ideal that harks back—even in its difference—to the stillness of German *Klassik*. Stasis serves the poet's personal goal of endurance amidst chaos and pain, but Benn, unlike the Stoics, restricts harmonic repose to the purely private sphere. By embracing stasis over *Bewegung*, he adds a new dimension to the concept of political *Ruhe*, while at the same time perpetuating nonprogressive structures visible throughout the history of German quietude and interiority.

We viewed Benn's poems within the context of that complex phenomenon known as the inner emigration, which was discussed primarily as an elevation of stillness and transhistorical truth that attempted to counter the national socialist valuation of the expedient, the momentary, and the powerful. National socialism can be viewed as a form of relativism that enables arbitrary acts of tyranny. Writers of the inner emigration, among them Benn, recognized this structure but—for various reasons—did not develop their insights beyond the moment of abstract reflection.

Rather than grounding my critique of Benn's concept of stasis (along with his earlier support of national socialism) on the fact that my views of life and literature are different from his and that he has failed to meet an externally imposed standard, I have attempted to demonstrate that many of his ideas conflict with their own presuppositions and so cancel themselves. These philosophical weaknesses do not erase the value of Benn's static poetry; his evocations of wholeness and harmony, of abiding values and genuine selfhood, demand admiration even as he tries, unsuccessfully, to overcome nihilism and reach the universal through decisionistic and formalist means alone.

My response to Benn's poems is, in summary, ambivalent. The four works analyzed here are excellently crafted texts, rich with hidden meanings both in their formal structures and in their multifarious intellectual-historical allusions. The poems contain individual insights of transhistorical relevance, which the references to $\dot{\alpha}\nu\dot{\alpha}\mu\nu\eta\sigma\iota\varsigma$ and the allusions to earlier thinkers cleverly reinforce. Benn's answer to nihilism, which culminates in the concept of the static poem, is, however, insufficient to its own purpose and internally contradictory. Nonetheless, I take this yearning for stasis to be an intuitively correct desire for transcendence and an understandable longing to carve a space for himself beyond the world of disorientation and injustice. Just as Benn's inner emigration is in part admirable, in part insufficient, so too his embrace of stasis—and, given a definition of art that is not arbitrary and so does not exclude truth, so too the poems themselves.

Notes

Chapter 1

1. Rilke would also lend himself to a monograph on stillness. Though Rilke and Benn share a positive reception of stillness, two points of difference might be noted. First, Rilke consistently affirms a *dynamic* stillness, and with this, transformation and change (see especially his *Sonette an Orpheus*), whereas Benn increasingly elevates stasis and does so in part at the expense of dynamism. Second, Rilke associates *Ruhe* with a condition desirable for humankind but ultimately beyond our reach (hence his many references to plants and his affirmation of a religious tradition that attributes stillness to divinity); this contrasts with Benn's suggestion that humans, in particular the poet and the sage, do indeed attain stillness.

2. For general commentary on Benn's concept of *Statik* see especially Steinhagen, *Statische Gedichte*, and Theo Meyer, 76–91. Less helpful, though not completely without insight, is the dissertation by Reichel.

3. Of the four poems I analyze, only the two middle works, "Wer allein ist—" and "Statische Gedichte," were actually published in the collection *Statische Gedichte*.

4. See Steinhagen, *Statische Gedichte*, 244–45.

5. Critics, restricting the origins of *Statik* to the natural sciences, have overlooked the technical usage of the term in Weimar legal philosophy—for example, in Kelsen, where *Statik* and *Dynamik* designate, respectively, "Die Geltung der Staatsordnung" and "Die Entstehung der Staatsordnung." There are thus precedents for Benn's association of *Statik* with what is synchronic or ahistorical, even if, as in his reformulation of the scientific connotations of *Statik*, he gives the word a new dimension.

6. The one exception is my discussion of the political connotations of *Statik*, which leads to a revision of our understanding of Benn's relationship to inner emigration.

7. Since readers of this book are likely to know German, I have not burdened the text with translations of quoted passages. For anyone interested in teaching these poems in English, translations of two of the four are available as follows: "Wer allein ist—" (R, 113–14; S, 213–15, 276–77); and "Reisen" (R, 118–19; S, 247, 283–84). Individual stanzas of "Statische Gedichte" have been translated in the secondary literature, but I have yet to see a complete translation. "Trunkene Flut" has, to my knowledge, never been translated.

8. Besides selecting the works for their illustration of Benn's developing conception of stasis, the density of their intellectual-historical allusions, and their varied, though equally elegant, formal structures, I have endeavored to choose examples from among poems that are often reprinted and thus fre-

quently taught, even if the poems selected are perhaps less often taught than Benn's more dissonant works.

9. For detailed information on the interesting prehistory of *Ruhe*, see my earlier study *Dynamic Stillness*.

10. Hillebrand introduces a representative selection of Benn criticism by stating, "Die meisten Beiträge gehen literaturimmanent vor" (5). Among the sociological readings, Schröder's studies from 1978 and 1986 are especially perceptive. In his recommendation for future scholarship Wodtke notes that "Benns Zusammenhang mit den abendländischen Geistestraditionen" has been neglected (*Gottfried Benn*, 106). The few noteworthy contributions to Benn criticism from this vantage point are Brode, "Studien" of 1972 and 1973, and Wodtke, "Die Antike." Homeyer also approaches Benn by way of his relationship to intellectual history, though her contribution brings fewer particular insights.

11. It is this concern with logical coherence as an element of beauty that will lead me to include an excursus on national socialism and transcendental norms, as I approach, and attempt to ground, my critique of Benn.

Chapter 2

1. See, e.g., *GW*, 2:300.

2. The poet aligns himself with Nietzsche's anti-Hegelian view, according to which the lyricist transcends subjectivity: "Das 'Ich' des Lyrikers tönt also aus dem Abgrunde des Seins: seine 'Subjektivität' im Sinne der neueren Ästhetiker ist eine Einbildung . . . Insofern aber das Subjekt Künstler ist, ist es bereits von seinem individuellen Willen erlöst und gleichsam Medium geworden, durch das hindurch eine wahrhaft seiende Subjekt seine Erlösung im Scheine feiert" (1:37, 40).

3. The passage is clearly influenced by Lucien Lévy-Bruhl's *Fonctions mentales dans les sociétés inférieures*, a work Benn knew in German translation and from which he quotes in his contemporary "Zur Problematik des Dichterischen" (*GW*, 1:76–77).

4. In the dominant myths, it is Hermes and not Demeter who descends into Hades to rescue Persephone. The reference "steigt Demeter" could thus be symbolic: with the literal ascension of Persephone, Demeter, representing the sphere of the earth, symbolically ascends; the earth blossoms. It could also signify, as with other instances later in the poem, Benn's desire to alter the chronological and spatial components of myth, a desire whose source and *telos* is a sense of undivided unity. A precedent for this would be the frequent overlapping of Demeter and Persephone in traditional mythology. Cf. Rohde, 1:211–12. However, the matter is probably much simpler. There is an older and lesser-known version of the myth (represented in the forty-first Orphic hymn and in the myth of Dysaules) according to which Demeter herself descends into Hades to retrieve Persephone. Ovid alludes to this tradition, without himself following it, both in *Metamorphoses* (5:533) and in *Fasti* (4:612). Cf. Malten, 533, and Kerényi, 422.

5. Benn describes Dionysus as being "umschwärmt von Mänaden in Fuchspelz und gehörnt" (*GW*, 1:20).
6. See especially Reinhold Grimm, *Gottfried Benn*, 41–49.
7. The poet may want us, at least at this point, to think of both Prometheus and Christ. In Benn's poem "Die Dänin" the two figures are explicitly viewed as parallel (*GW*, 3:103–6). Cf. Lohner, 158.
8. See also "Gedichte": "Am Steingeröll der großen Weltruine, dem Ölberg, wo die tiefste Seele litt . . ." (*GW*, 3:196).
9. Cf. Benn's comments on Prometheus's suffering in a letter to Käthe von Porada from 7 September 1933: "Europa ist der Erdteil der Abgründe u der Schatten, denken Sie doch, daß im hellsten Griechenland Prometheus an den Felsen mußte u. *wie* er litt!" (*T*, 138).
10. For Benn the most significant symbol of mankind is the suffering individual, and it is primarily the poet's extreme suffering that allows him to identify with the gods. See especially "Dennoch die Schwerter halten" (*GW*, 3:182) and "Gedichte" (*GW*, 3:196). See also Benn's quotation of Balzac, "Wer Dichtung sagt, sagt Leid" (*GW*, 1:307).
11. See Rohde's *Psyche*, 2:3 and 2:32–35, a text with which Benn was familiar (*GW*, 2:133).
12. The pertinent passage in "Pallas" reads: "Pallas . . . sieht Apollon, den Gefährten der Szene, und ihr fällt die Bemerkung des Proteus ein, des Beherrschers der Meerkälber, daß an dieser Stelle nicht weit vor, nach Götterstunden gerechnet, ein anderer stehen würde, um die Auferstehung der Toten zu verkünden" (*GW*, 1:368).
13. The poet will identify with Odysseus's entreaty of the dead once again in "Quartär" (*GW*, 3:185–87).
14. Benn's poem also echoes Rimbaud's famous poem of 1871, "Le bateau ivre," with its intertwining of the imagery of intoxication, water, unity, and death, its dissolution of the finite, and its exploratory, almost random, vision of unreal images and spaces (Rimbaud, 128–31).
15. See Brode, "Studien . . . II," 296–98. Brode, however, doesn't recognize the significance of *die Mütter* for Benn before 1930.
16. On the complexity of the relationship between sacrifice and self-preservation see Heimann.
17. The only difference is that "fleckt" appears in the opening lines as part of a compound: "trance- und traumgefleckt."
18. On the increasing erasure of the finite verb in Benn's lyrics—first, as an effort to avoid logical propositions, and second, as an attempt to convey stasis—see Seidler.
19. See, for example, Proclus, *The Elements of Theology*, props. 33 and 146; Pseudo-Dionysus, *Divine Names*, 4:8–9 = 704D–705B, and 4:14 = 712D–713A; Cusanus, *De possest*, especially 18:1–24:22; and more recently, Goethe, "Wenn im Unendlichen dasselbe" (1:367), and Schiller, "Die Worte des Glaubens" (*Gedichte*, 157). Consider also Benn's own stress on circularity in his later definition of "Statische Metaphysik" (*GW*, 2:158).
20. To borrow from Krieger's expanded definition of the figure of *ekphrasis* or the imitation in literature of a work of plastic art, we can say that Benn's

poem "takes on the 'still' elements of plastic form which we normally attribute to the spatial arts" (6).

21. Nemerov plays on this ambiguity frequently; see, for example, 6, 22, 97, 137, 216, 231, and 440.

22. The poet, as a suffering figure in the age of art, is representative of modern humanity in the same way that Christ was representative of humanity in the age of religion. See the informative discussion of Benn's *imitatio* (or *usurpatio*) *Christi* in Schröder, *Benn und die Deutschen*, 39–57.

23. See Lohner, 212.

24. See, for example, Schiller, "Das Ideal und das Leben" (*Gedichte*, 135–40) or Hölderlin, "An den Aether" (1:204–5).

25. In Nietzsche's anomalous, though influential, reading of the Greek gods, Apollo is associated with the world of dreams (1:21–24).

26. In this context consider Benn's affirmation of the stillness in moving things: "Die Woge, die auf u nieder geht, veränderlich u. doch identisch, Sansaras Rad, das sich dreht, doch nicht bewegt, sind tiefere Symbole" (*Oelze* no. 110 [6 December 1936]).

27. Wodtke sees three stages in Benn's poetic development, in each of which a certain mythological figure, together with the cluster of ideas he represents, predominates: first, Dionysus; second, Orpheus; third, Apollo. "Trunkene Flut," though primarily Dionysian, clearly moves in the direction of the Orphic motif of revival, and even in the direction of Apollinian closure.

Chapter 3

1. See Theo Meyer, 327.

2. Nietzsche writes in *Die Philosophie im tragischen Zeitalter der Griechen* that Heraclitus's world "zeigt nirgends ein Verharren, eine Unzerstörbarkeit, ein Bollwerk im Strome" (3:369).

3. Cf. *GW*, 4:185. The original can be found in Diels and Kranz, 154, no. 12.

4. Cf. similarly *GW*, 3:161. With his stress on the poet's (almost heroic) ability to stand amidst the flow (and confusion) of everyday life, Benn reemploys—without adopting its clear religious and ethical implications—a significant Baroque motif. See, for example, Gryphius, *Catharina von Georgien*, I, 813, and IV, 527. For a general discussion of the frequency of Baroque elements in the opposition poetry of the inner emigration see Hoffmann, *Opposition Poetry*, 165–66.

5. On geology as the transformation of history in Benn see Allemann, especially 36–44.

6. Cf. Benn's own statement in *Doppelleben*: "Kunst . . . hebt die Zeit und die Geschichte auf" (*GW*, 4:129).

7. Benn links *Statik* with emotionlessness when he speaks of a "Wiederkehr . . . zum Statischen u. Affektlosen" (*Oelze* no. 188 [3 November 1940]).

8. In "Können Dichter die Welt ändern?" Benn states: "Kunstwerke sind phänomenal, historisch unwirksam, praktisch folgenlos. Das ist ihre Größe" (*GW*, 4:215). Not only does the artist not *desire* an effect (the artist is not bound by an external *telos*), the lack of an effect is art's greatness (art has, in principle, even for the viewer, no purpose).
9. On similarities between Rilke's Malte and Benn's Rönne see Theo Meyer, 193.
10. For a comparison of the two poems see Brackert.
11. Earlier titles for Goethe's "Selige Sehnsucht" were "Selbstopfer" and "Vollendung" (2:582). Both concepts are present in Benn's poem, though in ways extraordinarily different from their use in Goethe's poem.
12. For a different realization of the concept that great artworks are "all eye," see Rilke's well-known poem "Archaïscher Torso Apollos," which concludes with the lines: "denn da ist keine Stelle, / die dich nicht sieht. Du mußt dein Leben ändern."
13. On Benn's proximity to romanticism in other respects see Reichel, "Die 'Statischen Gedichte,'" 148–49.
14. In the context of his affirmation of anti-Faustian or static poetry Benn likes to quote from Goethe's sonnet "Natur und Kunst," with its affirmation of "Beschränkung" and "Gesetz" and its assertion: "Vergebens werden ungebundene Geister / Nach der Vollendung reiner Höhe streben" (1:245). See Benn's letters to Peter Schifferli of 23 November 1947 (*DD*, 93) and to Armin Mohler of 26 November 1949 (*B*, 182).
15. "Aber da eine letzte Grenze vorhanden, so ist es vollendet von (und nach) allen Seiten, einer wohlgerundeten Kugel Maße vergleichbar, von der Mitte her überall gleichgewichtig" (Diels and Kranz, 238, no. 8).
16. Benn's embrace of stasis has a philosophical dimension that relates to contemporary as much as to classical philosophy. His position functions as a critique of an early twentieth-century German philosophy developed in the wake of Nietzsche that recognizes only motion and flux, while denying the existence of an absolute or its symbolic corollary stillness. The following passages from Semi Meyer's *Geistige Wirklichkeit* might serve as an illustration: "Die Welt ist nicht innerlich ruhig und nur an der Oberfläche bewegt, sondern Bewegung ist ihr innerstes Wesen, ihr ganzes Sein, ihre ganze, volle und auch ihre letzte Wirklichkeit. Ruhe ist das Nichts, nur Bewegung und Regung ist etwas" (7); "Der immer noch beliebten Bewertung des Dauernden oder gar des Ewigen ist mit aller Entschiedenheit und Kraft zu widersprechen. Wir sind Geschöpfe der Zeitlichkeit und haben im Überzeitlichen nichts zu suchen . . . Alles Leben ist im Fluß und nichts hat darin Platz, was nicht im Strom des Werdens und Wandels sich bewährt. Das aber kann nichts Unveränderliches. Der Geist gehört dem Leben an, und über dem Leben kann es schon gewiß für den Menschen nichts geben" (258–59). (For the context of these passages, see Meyer, 1–9 and 253–60.) Interesting in their contrast to Benn's delineation of stillness and stasis are two additional points: Meyer's assertion of an all-pervasive causality ("Wirkung in sich selbst ist undenkbar" [3]), along with his corollary denial of any stable *Ruhe*;

and his explicitly anti-Greek (anti-Platonic in the critique of ideal forms, anti-Aristotelian in the denial of an unmoved mover) and anti-Asian rhetoric (6–8, 254–58). Meyer's study was among the works Benn owned at the time of his death. I am grateful to Ilse Benn for letting me copy this list in the summer of 1984.

17. See, for example, Herder, 8:65; Schiller, *Werke*, 20:472; Hölderlin, 3:126; and Richter, 5:78.

18. "Es gelten nur die abgeschlossenen Gebilde, die Statuen, die Friese, der Schild des Achill, diese sind ohne Ideen, sagen nur sich selbst und sind vollendet" (*GW*, 1:368–69). Cf. *GW*, 4:434–37.

Chapter 4

1. In a sketch Benn had used the term "Entwicklungfeindschaft" (*SW*, 1:477)—a word he later eliminated, one assumes, because it suggests emotion and negation rather than indifference.

2. There is an interesting biographical corollary to this position. Benn writes in 1946: "Für Kinder interessiere ich mich ja nicht, auch nicht mal für die meiner Tochter" (*T*, 109).

3. Cf. "Clemenceau": " 'nichts ist wahr. Alles ist wahr. / Das ist der Weisheit letzter Schluß' " (*GW*, 3:442).

4. Benn's withdrawal, viewed as a negation of historical disintegration, exhibits similarities with the Stoic world view. Hegel writes: "Denn wenn die Realität der Welt verlorengegangen wie in der römischen Welt, der reale Geist, das Leben im abstrakten Allgemeinen verschwunden, muß das Bewußtsein, dessen reale Allgemeinheit zerstört ist, in seine Einzelheit zurückgehen und in seinen Gedanken sich selbst erhalten . . . Es liegt hierin die Bestimmung der abstrakten Freiheit, der abstrakten Unabhängigkeit" (19:293–94). Hegel goes on to criticize this elevation of the private as internally contradictory, as a formal morality void of content, and as a harmony that is exclusive and therefore not truly harmonic. He concludes with words that could also apply, *mutatis mutandis*, to Benn: "Es liegt also darin, nicht daß der Zustand der Welt ein vernünftiger, ein rechtlicher sei, sondern nur das Subjekt als solches soll seine Freiheit in sich behaupten . . . Die edlen Römer haben daher nur das Negative bewiesen, diese Gleichgültigkeit gegen Leben, gegen alles Äußerliche; sie haben nur auf subjektive oder negative Weise groß sein können, in Weise eines Privatmannes" (19:294, 296). (Cf. 17:266–69.) That there are more and less intersubjective variants of Stoicism need not concern us here.

5. Many of Benn's quietistic statements could be compared with thoughts expressed in the *Tao Te Ching*: for example, the elevation of not-doing (3), nonaction (43, 48), nondesire (64), and nothingness (38); the evocation of serenity (9) and of calm (64), as well as of a center (5, 19, 29, 53); and the embrace of the unchanging (25) and the unmoved (26).

6. A very different reception of the sage and of Asian wisdom is present in

Brecht, one of the twentieth century's most outspoken critics of *Ruhe*. In his "Legende von der Entstehung des Buches Taoteking auf dem Weg des Laotse in die Emigration," Brecht writes on behalf of Lao-tzu: "Daß das weiche Wasser in Bewegung / Mit der Zeit den mächtigen Stein besiegt. / Du verstehst, das Harte unterliegt" (9:660). Also in contrast to Benn is the stress in Brecht's poem on the communication and mediation of wisdom.

7. The relativist position involves a contradiction between the statement's form—with its claim to truth—and its content—with its erasure of truth. Later in this study I will present a fuller discussion of such contradictions and a critique of Benn's doctrine of stasis. Here one might simply reflect on the aesthetic merit of a position whose form and content—in this broader sense—fail to harmonize.

8. For Benn's interest in this doctrine see, e.g., GW, 1:343, 2:163, 2:240, and 2:282.

9. See Pliny, *Historia Naturalis*, 35:160. Benn was of course familiar with this tradition; see "V. Jahrhundert" (*GW*, 3:201).

10. See Nietzsche, 2:135, 221–22, 599, 647, 860–61; 3:441, 705–6, 903; and elsewhere. Cf. *Oelze* no. 2 (27 January 1933).

11. Benn cites these concepts in his essay "Sein und Werden" (*GW*, 4:253).

12. "Mit dem Worte 'das Unhistorische' bezeichne ich die Kunst und Kraft *vergessen* zu können und sich in einen begrenzten *Horizont* einzuschließen; 'überhistorisch' nenne ich die Mächte, die den Blick von dem Werden ablenken, hin zu dem, was dem Dasein den Charakter des Ewigen und Gleichbedeutenden gibt, zu *Kunst* und *Religion*" (Nietzsche, 1:281).

13. I refer, of course, to the science and art of linear perspective, first developed in Florence in the fifteenth century.

14. See Theo Meyer, 85.

15. Cf. Manyoni, 226.

16. The negation of life, including flux and suffering, via art and stillness brings Benn in close proximity to Schopenhauer: see Schopenhauer, especially 2:468–92, 504–8; 4:670–89, 706–43. A great deal has been written on Nietzsche and Benn, but the nineteenth-century writer who appears to have the most in common with Benn is Schopenhauer. Many of the positions Benn shares with Nietzsche derive from Schopenhauer, and the positions he adopts in countering Nietzsche bring him back to Schopenhauer. All three thinkers privilege art, question historical optimism, and scorn eudemonism, but only Schopenhauer and Benn associate aesthetic experience with transcendence and a rejection of the dynamism and superficiality of life. In Benn, as earlier in Schopenhauer, we see the abandonment of will, action, and experience in favor of artistic contemplation; an evocation of the mystical *nunc stans*; the adoption of quietism; the elevation of nothingness; and an earnest reception of Oriental literature and philosophy. Surprisingly, there is no comprehensive study of Schopenhauer and Benn.

17. For example, *GW*, 1:83, 1:360, and 4:308; *Oelze* no. 43 (16 September 1935) and no. 45 (7 October 1935).

18. See, e.g., *GW*, 2:139.

19. The one other use of "sinken lassen" in Benn with which I am familiar underscores this reading, even as it views inward movement more dynamically (as would be appropriate for a text written closer to the genesis of "Trunkene Flut"). In "Zur Problematik des Dichterischen" Benn writes: "Daß er [the poet] dies alles hinter sich läßt, die Perspektive seiner Herkunft und Verantwortung weiterrückt bis dahin, wo die logischen Systeme ganz vergehn, sich tiefer sinken läßt in einer Art Rückfallfieber und Sturzgeburt nach innen" (GW, 1:76).

20. The poem, however, does reach its readers. The idea of a monologic art is self-canceling and must pass over into either silence or communication. In this general direction cf. Reichel, *Künstlermoral*, 59, 68; and Gerth, 243–44.

Chapter 5

1. See Fick, 87.

2. "Reisen" shares a general critique of travel—as well as the specific implication that in traveling one is a slave to bodily, not intellectual, needs—with Opitz's "Sta Viator!" The latter poem, like "Reisen," begins with two rhetorical questions: "Ihr blinden Sterblichen, was zieht ihr und verreist / Nach beiden Indien? Was wagt ihr Seel und Geist / Für ihren Knecht, den Leib?" The gold the travelers seek is in their own hands: "Ihr pflügt die wilde See, vergesset euer Land, / Sucht Gold, das eisern macht, und habt es bei der Hand." The poet concludes, again like Benn, with a form of the verb *bleiben*: "Hierher, Mensch! Die Natur, die Erde rufet dir. / Wohin? Nach Gute? Bleib! Warum? Du hast es hier!" There are, of course, significant differences between the two poems. In brief, Opitz embraces not the self but the wider intersubjective sphere of "euer Land"; he appeals not to a nebulous *Sie* but to a specific audience, the traveler; he suggests a definite goal for the traveler, "das Gute"; and he concludes with an imperative, not a syntactically estranged infinitive.

3. See also *DW*, 1:171, 193; 2:77; 3:21; and 5:254. I have selected the following example because it echoes not only Aquinas's important argument from physical motion but also the Aristotelian concept of the unmoved mover that will concern us later. The reception of this Aristotelian notion was widespread in German mysticism. See, for example, Suso, 388. For examples of Suso's and Tauler's use of the terms "wŭste" and "wŭstenunge" see Suso, 245, and Tauler, 406.

4. What reinforces the suspected association with Eckhart is the fact that Eckhart elevates subjectivity and solitude, as does Benn in this poem, to an extraordinary degree: "Sehet, der mensche, der alsô éin sun ist, der nimet bewegunge und würkunge und allez, das er nimet,—daz nimet er allez in sînem eigene . . . suln des menschen werk leben, sô müezen sie genomen werden von sînem eigene, niht von vremden dingen noch ûzer im, sunder in im" (*DW*, 2:383–84).

5. Eckhart's and Silesius's views on stillness reach back to the philosophy

of Epicurus and the Bible. Epicurus's follower Lucretius, for example, writes that to receive the divine, we must be like the gods—that is, we must possess a tranquillity of spirit (5:1198–1203; 6:43–78). In the Judaeo-Christian tradition the individual who wants to receive the divine in his or her soul must be "still before the Lord and wait patiently for him" (Ps. 37:7); cf. Ps. 62:1; Isa. 30:15; Lam. 3:26.

6. Though Geneva would have proffered a more precise allusion to Calvinism, it might have evoked too many competing, and for the poem perhaps unproductive, associations. In this context it may be worthwhile to note that Benn's mother came from Switzerland and that his father was a Protestant minister.

7. Melin and Zorach trace images of Cuba in German literature. Though they do not mention Benn, they do discuss Cuba as a travel destination for seekers of the exotic life. For a general discussion of the travel theme in Benn, see Bielefeld.

8. One might quote here Benn himself: "Es darf nichts zufällig sein in einem Gedicht" (GW, 1:524).

9. My reading of Zurich represents in part the outcome of a lively and helpful discussion, at the 1987 Kentucky Foreign Language Conference, following a paper I gave entitled "Gottfried Benn's Poem 'Reisen' in Its Intellectual-Historical Context."

10. The contrast presupposes a literal reading of the second stanza of "Statische Gedichte," that is, as an affirmation of idyllic existence.

11. Streets are presented in German, French, English, and Dutch. Note Benn's selection of the most elegant possibilities—for example, boulevards. *Lido* is Italian for "seashore" or "beach."

12. There appears to be an allusion here—by way of "Bahnhofstraßen," and especially "Fifth Avenues"—to materialism. Travel and materialism are not infrequently linked. Cf. Linda Schulte-Sasse, 41–42.

13. Cf. the force of the above passage with the much simpler lines in "Melancholie": "Du mußt aus deiner Gegend alles holen, / denn auch von Reisen kommst du leer zurück" (GW, 3:303).

14. Cf. GW, 1:371.

15. For passages besides those that follow, see Seneca's *Letters*, nos. 2, 54, 55, 56, and *De tranquillitate animi*, 2:10–15 and 12. Benn discusses Seneca in Oelze no. 146 (6 July 1938) and elsewhere. See also Marcus Aurelius's *Meditations* (1:16; 2:7; 4:3; 12:8), with which Benn was also familiar (GW, 1:19, and Oelze no. 189 [24 November 1940]); and Lipsius, *De constantia*, 1:2–3 (in *Opera*, 4:527–30). Partly because of Lipsius's influence, Baroque writers viewed travel as a false escape from psychological (and ethical) turmoil. In addition to Opitz's "Sta Viator!" see, for example, Gryphius's *Papinian* (I, 135–36).

16. The translations of Seneca given in the text are those of Robin Campbell. "Animum debes mutare, non caelum . . . Quid terrarum iuvare novitas potest? Quid cognitio urbium aut locorum? In inritum cedit ista iactatio. Quaeris quare te fuga ista non adiuvet? Tecum fugis. Onus animi deponendum est; non ante tibi ullus placebit locus" (*Epistolae*, no. 28).

17. "Quid per se peregrinatio prodesse cuiquam potuit? . . . Non iudicium dedit, non discussit errorem, sed ut puerum ignota mirantem ad breve tempus rerum aliqua novitate detinuit. Ceterum inconstantia mentis, quae maxime aegra est, lacessit, mobiliorem levioremque reddit ipsa iactatio. Itaque, quae petierant cupidissime loca, cupidius deserunt et avium modo transvolant citiusque quam venerant, abeunt" (Seneca, *Epistolae*, no. 104).

18. Despite Benn's repeated insistence on pure form, there is in this poem a definite theme. In fact, even his purely formal poems attempt to thematize their formality in the same way that his specifically static poems thematize stillness. On the tension between Benn's poetics and his poetry, see Vahland; Schröder, *Benn und die Deutschen*, 58–72; and Willems, who sees in Benn's poems of the 1950s a decided break with esoteric formalism and a movement toward the representation of everyday reality.

19. Cf. Theo Meyer, 340.

20. The poet's choice of *vergeblich* is genuine, not ironic. There is no evidence of a causal connection between *fahren* and *erfahren*, not even in the sense—and here *vergeblich* would be ironic—that travel teaches the traveler the purposelessness of travel and so becomes, in a paradoxical sense, purposeful.

21. Cf. also Benn's "Totenrede für Klabund," where the poet suggests that self-fulfillment and truth lie "jenseits jeder Empirie" (*GW*, 1:408).

22. See Stifter, *Nachsommer*, 708–10. A delimiting of travel—at least from the perspective of space devoted to its description—is similarly at work in Stifter's "Heidedorf," a story in part about the development of a poetic consciousness. As additional evidence for the proximity of Stifter and Benn on travel, see the Major's recognition in *Brigitta* that travel leads nowhere; the narrator writes: "er sei jetzt endlich gesonnen, auf einem einzigen winzigen Punkte dieser Erdkugel kleben zu bleiben, und kein anderes Stäubchen mehr auf seinen Fuß gelangen zu lassen, als das der Heimat, in welcher er nunmehr ein Ziel gefunden habe, das er sonst vergeblich auf der ganzen Welt gesucht hatte" (4).

23. Cf. J. P. Stern, especially 119–22.

24. See Stifter, *Nachsommer*, 13 and 339–49. In Stifter, as later in Benn, we see a psychological corollary to aesthetic stillness, although for Stifter psychological tranquillity necessarily involves moral and social dimensions; see 228, 477, 660–63, and 680–82.

25. See Maurach, 209.

26. "Num quid tam turbidum fieri potest quam forum? Ibi quoque licet quiete vivere, si necesse sit" (Seneca, *Epistolae*, no. 28).

27. A biographically oriented reading along the lines of Schröder's study of Benn from 1978 would find support for a reading of "Grenze" as a form of *Abwehr*.

28. In distancing himself from Goethe, Benn nears the position of Schopenhauer, who cites Goethe's "Prometheus" as an illustration of total "Bejahung des Willens zum Leben" and contrasts it with a view closer to his own metaphysical position, namely the quietistic "Verneinung des Willens zum Leben"; see Schopenhauer, 2:358–59.

29. By focusing on the much earlier "Heinrich Mann. Ein Untergang," Schröder shows that Benn's view of Prometheus deviates from tradition insofar as Prometheus becomes for Benn an asocial figure; what Prometheus does, he does for himself, not humankind (see *Benn. Poesie*, 41). This of course brings the creator Prometheus in line with Benn's own view of the artist.

30. See *Physics*, 8, and *Metaphysics*, 12. A central passage reads: "There is, then, something which is always moved with an unceasing motion, which is motion in a circle; and this is plain not in theory only but in fact. Therefore the first heaven must be eternal. There is therefore also something which moves it. And since that which is moved and moves is intermediate, there is something which moves without being moved, being eternal, substance, and actuality" (*Metaphysics*, 12:7). The concept also plays a role in the fifth chapter of Bonaventure's *Itinerarium Mentis in Deum* (18).

31. If Benn did not take the concept of an unmoved mover from Aristotle or the Christian mystics, he may have been thinking of Plato, for whom the circular, self-sufficient union of rest and motion is a less central, if nonetheless distinct, concept. In the *Timaeus* Plato explains that God "made the universe a circle moving in a circle, one and solitary, yet by reason of its excellence able to converse with itself, and needing no other friendship or acquaintance" (34b). In Plato we also find the connection between self-motion and thought, a connection important for Benn not only in "Reisen" but in "Wer allein ist—" and "Statische Gedichte" as well: "Now of all motions that is the best which is produced in a thing by itself, for it is most akin to the motion of thought and of the universe" (*Timaeus*, 89a). Benn implies that it is not in travel but in self-sufficient repose that one finds the wondrous. This, too, harks back to the Platonic view. In the *Laws* Plato addresses the concept of immobile centers around which there are circles of motion and which, together, are "a source of all sorts of marvels" (893d). Plato equates the highest form of motion, that which moves itself, with the soul (896a). Because the individual self mirrors the soul as universal cause, it recognizes its unity with other selves. For Benn, on the other hand, the poetic *Ich* is not primarily equivalent but unique—not like, but unlike, other selves. Its frontier is a barrier. In Benn's framework the poetic self replaces, rather than identifies with, the divine soul(s). Instead of employing self-movement as proof of divine existence (or of transcendental truth), Benn invokes the concept to legitimate his unique poetic enterprise.

32. The image of poetic divinity alludes not only to classical antiquity; by way of its references to "Manna" and German mysticism, "Reisen" is also connected to the Judaeo-Christian tradition. Consider the German version of the opening of Genesis: "Am Anfang schuf Gott Himmel und Erde. Und die Erde war wüst und leer, und es war finster auf der Tiefe; und der Geist Gottes schwebte auf dem Wasser. Und Gott sprach: Es werde Licht! Und es ward Licht." One hears in these words the key concepts of "Reisen": *Wüste, Leere, Tiefe,* followed by God's act of creation. Out of chaos and emptiness God creates "L-ich-t." Benn, skeptical of religious faith along with enlightenment and intersubjective truth, creates instead only an "Ich." The poet forms

himself, that is, his identity, in his works and creates his works for himself. The poem would fulfill itself not in shedding light but in erasing the objectivity of its own message. In the nihilistic *Weinhaus Wolf*, Benn writes with another clear allusion to, and inversion of, the Biblical passage quoted above: "Der Geist liegt schweigend über den Wassern" (GW, 2:150).

33. Brode ("Studien . . . I") traces the meaning of circular metaphors throughout Benn's poetry. See also Casper.

34. The intellectual-historical allusions are thus revealed to be more than ornamental; they are a substantive element of a world view that Benn cultivates in contrast to a modernity concerned only with what is current and immediate, a modernity obsessed with external travel and superficialities, a modernity denied access to the golden bough: "Der Überlieferungslose, der Nichtgeist, der Moderne federt in den Welten herum, alles . . . zu bereisen, zu berieseln, zu beriechen" (GW, 4:256).

35. For Spengler's discussion of the Greek principle of limit, see especially 119–22; on the contrast of Apollinian *Statik* and Faustian *Dynamik* and—apropos of "Reisen"—on the Apollinian *Physik der Nähe* versus the Faustian *Physik der Ferne*, see 234–35, 389, 489–92, and 533–34. On Benn's general reception of Spengler see especially Brode, "Studien . . . I," 749–63.

Chapter 6

1. Owing either to his activities in 1933 or to the obliqueness of his verse, Benn is normally not included among discussions of the inner emigration. Ritchie's recent study of German literature between 1933 and 1945 illustrates this point. The one notable exception to this direction is Willems (10–12, 15–22).

2. See Alter, *Gottfried Benn*. Also of interest in this respect, if somewhat less detailed, is Steinhagen, "Gottfried Benn 1933."

3. Alter's claim is at least partially convincing, but he tends to downplay in contrast Benn's genuine enthusiasm for the "metaphysical" content of national socialism, and he is hard pressed to explain away, in the light of his own claims, Benn's attack on *Geistesfreiheit* in "Der neue Staat und die Intellektuellen."

4. See Jens, 189–228 and 290–94. Cf. Alter, *Gottfried Benn*, and Steinhagen, "Gottfried Benn 1933."

5. For an account of "National Socialism as Temptation," not just to Benn but to intellectuals in general, see Fritz Stern.

6. The allusion is to *Der preußische Stil*.

7. For a differentiated discussion of connections between Benn's elevation of form, his belief in biological *Züchtung*, and his affirmation of fascism, see Fischer.

8. Benn aligns the metaphysical with what is antirational: "Bis vor kurzem war der Mensch ein Vernunftswesen und sein Hirn der Vater aller Dinge, heute ist er ein metaphysisches Wesen, abhängig und von Ursprung und Natur umrahmt" (GW, 1:215). In his "Antwort an die literarischen Emigran-

ten" he contrasts "metaphysisch" with both "aufklärerisch" and "humanistisch" (*GW*, 4:241).

9. On decisionism see especially Krockow.

10. Cf. Alter, *Gottfried Benn*, 85.

11. This view, clearly espoused in "Die Eigengesetzlichkeit der Kunst" and "Die Dichtung braucht inneren Spielraum," differs from Benn's earlier statements in "Der neue Staat und die Intellektuellen."

12. The main trigger appears to have been the night of the long knives; see *B*, 58, and *Oelze* no. 101 (24 July 1934). However, the treatment accorded Benn by the National Socialists, above all Börries von Münchhausen, was also decisive. For general orientation see Wodtke, *Gottfried Benn*, 52–71; for detailed documentation see Alter, "Gottfried Benn."

13. My analysis of Benn's initial immersion in and later abandonment of national socialism focuses on his evaluation of the movement's intellectual content. Similarly, my critique will be directed at his ideas rather than any biographical reasons for his adoption of these ideas. However, I do not want to deny that Benn's affirmation of national socialism and his turn away from it may have been informed by biographical—that is, political and historical—rather than purely intellectual and philosophical reasons. During the first year after Hitler assumed power, the Nazis were uncertain how to deal with expressionism and with surviving expressionists such as Benn. As long as the Nazis tolerated Benn, he supported them. When they abandoned their tolerance (or ambivalence) toward the movement and began to attack Benn, the poet fled into the army, a move he inappropriately and absurdly termed "eine aristokratische Form der Emigrierung" (*B*, 62). Circumstantial evidence could lead one to conclude that Benn provided the appropriate philosophical underpinnings for his actions ex post facto, depending on his personal situation. For historical purposes this biographical dimension and the possibility of opportunism deserve consideration; however, as I will suggest below, it is of more universal interest to undermine not mere opportunism but the philosophical defense Benn attempts for his position, whatever its motivation.

14. *B*, 61. Cf. *Oelze* no. 19 (30 January 1935), and *GW*, 4:259.

15. Cf. Hoffmann, *Opposition Poetry* and "Opposition," 136.

16. Benn's poems represent of course the author's *internal* working through of his position vis-à-vis national socialism. Owing to his having been expelled from the *Reichschriftumskammer* in March 1938, his poems, distributed privately in the 1940s, were published only *after* the fall of national socialism. They were thus not part of the actual resistance. Benn's situation was not unique: much of the critical literature of the time was unpublished, including, for example, the important literary diaries of the day.

17. The most recent and comprehensive review of the various definitions and evaluations of the concept "inner emigration" is Schnell, *Literarische Innere Emigration*, 1–15. The best approach to the problem today would seem to be the analysis of individual works by individual authors in the light of the form, level, purpose, or effectiveness of opposition.

18. The two writers' correspondence is reprinted in Arnold, 1:247–68. For

Mann, see especially 253; for Thieß, see especially 248, 258, and 259.

19. Cf. Kant, *Kritik der reinen Vernunft*, B 371 (in *Werke*, 3:323). In "Antwort an die literarischen Emigranten" Benn employs the very same structure of argument by experience, rather than reason, in his *defense* of national socialism.

20. In this direction see also Loewy, 27–31; Brekle, 32–38; and Hoffmann, "Opposition."

21. Cf. Reinhold Grimm, "Im Dickicht," 411.

22. Benn's break with national socialism is clearer in his essays: "Züchtung II" (1940), "Kunst und drittes Reich" (1941), and "Zum Thema Geschichte" (ca. 1942–43).

23. See chapter 8 below.

24. See Schwerte, 8–9 and 148–90.

25. On the national socialist reception of *Faust* see, besides Schwerte, Belgum.

26. Ironically, the national socialist Benn contributed to the nazification of Faust; see *GW*, 1:222.

27. Of some interest in this context is Hitler's alleged remark: "Ich liebe Goethe nicht. Aber um des einen Wortes willen bin ich bereit, ihm vieles nachzusehen: 'Im Anfang war die Tat' " (Rauschning, 211). Cf. Heyse, 349.

28. Benn owned an edition from 1933.

29. For a statement of Rosenberg's impact, one might consider the words of Goebbels, speaking in the presence of Hitler in 1937: "Alfred Rosenberg hat in seinen Werken in hervorragendem Maße die Weltanschauung des Nationalsozialismus wissenschaftlich und intuitiv begründen und festigen geholfen . . . Erst eine spätere Zeit wird voll zu ermessen vermögen, wie tief der Einfluß dieses Mannes auf die geistige und weltanschauliche Gestaltung des nationalsozialistischen Reiches ist" (Härtle, 45). The fact that Rosenberg's power within the regime was often contested does not fundamentally diminish his influence on national socialist ideology. For a thorough evaluation of Rosenberg's influence, see Baumgärtner; also Hutchinson, especially 35–62 and 314–42.

30. Unless otherwise indicated, quotations from Rosenberg stem from *Der Mythus des 20. Jahrhunderts*.

31. "Griechische Schönheit ist also stets ein statisches, nicht dynamisches Wesen" (Rosenberg, 305).

32. Another dimension of the Rosenberg-Benn comparison is Rosenberg's elevation of Meister Eckhart as the precursor of a Nordic racial religion characterized by dynamism (see 216–59, especially 252), whereas for Benn, Eckhart is the model, as we saw in "Reisen," for a life of individual enclosure and stillness. The contrast, however, is complicated by Rosenberg's elevation of the solitude, seclusion, and privacy of the soul (for example, 232–35 and 252), indicating a common element in the two men's reception of Eckhart: the elevation of subjectivity over intersubjectivity.

33. Cf. Rosenberg, 271–72.

34. See especially Rosenberg, 315–22 and 405–52.

35. Rosenberg, *Letzte Aufzeichnungen*, 70.

36. For references to Lao-tzu see, for example, *GW*, 2:240, 4:68, and 4:254; *Oelze* no. 156 (11 December 1938) and no. 301 (19 February 1946); and *T*, 213.

37. Bayerdörfer takes the tension between the formal and political dimensions of poetry to be *"die* lyrikgeschichtliche Signatur seit der Weimarer Republik" (453).

38. See, for example, *GW*, 1:248, 442, 444, 446, 450; 4:397. On the importance of the concept *Bewegung* within national socialism cf. Klemperer, 237–42; Berning (1960), 88; and Berning (1961), 182.

39. Besides Rosenberg, other national socialist philosophers elevated the concepts of motion and dynamism and viewed them as specifically German. In his thoroughgoing polemic against philosophical rationalism and universalism, *Anti-Cartesianismus*, Franz Böhm includes a section entitled "Die Dynamik deutscher Philosophie" (158–74), in which he elevates activism, dynamism, and productive unrest. Benn's citations of Stoicism and Schopenhauer along with his elevation of inactivity might be contrasted with the following quotation from Böhm: "Deshalb 'beruhigt' auch keine deutsche Philosophie wie der Rationalismus der Stoa, Descartes oder Spinoza, die Systemdialektik Hegels oder der voluntaristische Nihilismus Schopenhauers beruhigen. Die Erkenntnis als 'Quietiv' des Willens stammt nicht aus Bereitschaft zum Mitvollzug der Wirklichkeit, sondern umgekehrt aus intellektueller Weigerung, das Schicksal der Wirklichkeit zu teilen" (163). In this context one might also note the following comments from Rauschning's *Gespräche mit Hitler*: "Der Mensch ist zum Handeln da. Nur als ein handelndes Wesen erfüllt er seine natürliche Bestimmung. Kontemplative Naturen, retrospektiv wie alle Geistigen, sind Tote, die den Sinn des Lebens verfehlen. Gerade wir Deutschen, die wir solange in Gedanken und Träumen ausschweiften, mußten zu der großen Wahrheit zurückfinden, daß nur die Tat und die ewige Bewegung dem menschlichen Leben Sinn geben. Jede Tat ist sinnvoll, selbst das Verbrechen. Jede Passivität, jedes Beharren ist dagegen sinnlos, sie sind lebensfeindlich. Somit gibt es das göttliche Recht, das Beharrende zu vernichten" (211).

40. For discussions of national socialist poetry see Bormann, Fredsted, Gamm, Geißler, Hartung, Ketelsen ("Nationalsozialismus und Drittes Reich"), and Loewy.

41. Kober, 17.

42. *Liederbuch der NSDAP*, 9.

43. See, for example, Langenbucher, 191.

44. One can include here Benn himself, who in "Der neue Staat und die Intellektuellen" heralded "eine Jugend . . . von verwandelter geschichtlicher Art . . . große, innerlich geführte Jugend" (*GW*, 1:447, 449).

45. The film's audience was reportedly well over twenty million; see Baird, 511.

46. Böhme, 360.

47. Willems draws attention to similarities between Benn and the poets of the inner emigration by discussing Benn's thematization of nature and

his neoclassical attention to form (17–21). The argument has some validity, though the two elements can also be discussed in the light of national socialist poetry.

48. For related themes in Hagelstange's sonnets see especially *Venezianisches Credo*, 27, 34, and 38.

49. The negation of universal truth, as we will see in the next chapter, runs throughout Rosenberg's *Mythus*, but see especially 22–23, 78–79, 117–37, 285–89, 390, 539, and 681–701.

50. In one of his more interesting sonnets Hagelstange works with a similar dualism; see *Venezianisches Credo*, 24.

51. Cf. Chick.

52. This is not to discount other factors that contributed to Benn's nonemigration, not the least of which was the author's initial infatuation with nazism. His reasons for not emigrating are spelled out in *Doppelleben*: first, the concept of emigration was not known in Germany at the time; second, Hitler came to power legally; third, no one took the national socialist program seriously (*GW*, 4:69–71). De Mendelssohn discusses some of the problems in Benn's reasoning; see 260–73.

53. Hoffmann, "Opposition," 131.

54. Fundamental on this issue is Schröder, *Benn. Poesie*.

55. This is not to suggest that one cannot—by way of Hermann Broch's account of partial value systems—read *l'art pour l'art* primarily (and independently of Benn) as a means of stabilization, the restriction of all significance to a finite, isolated sphere.

56. See "Antwort an die literarischen Emigranten," in which Benn fails to recognize motivations for emigration and nonemigration that transcend loyalty and endurance—such as, for example, adherence to principles of justice.

57. Cf. Roche, *Dynamic Stillness*, 163–71.

58. The classic formulation of the literature of inner emigration as reflection on what is eternal and timeless, and thus as flight into what is necessarily empty, is Schonauer: "Die Literatur der sogenannten inneren Emigration war Flucht. Flucht in die Idylle oder in die sogenannten einfachen und zeitlos menschlichen Verhältnisse, Flucht in den Traditionalismus, in die forcierte Betonung des alten Wahren und Unvergänglichen, Flucht in das Bewährte und damit Problemlose, Flucht nicht zuletzt vor der Trivialität und der Barbarei in das Schöne, Edle und Ewige" (127). The position has been upheld, with only slight modification, in the most extensive treatment of inner emigration to date; see Schnell, *Literarische Innere Emigration*—and Schnell, "Innere Emigration."

59. Cf. Roche, *Dynamic Stillness*, especially 121–23 and 249–50.

60. If Büchner and Heine, as I argued in *Dynamic Stillness*, turn to the historical in recognizing that the truth of the eternal principles symbolized in stillness is their *realization*, the writers of the inner emigration turn back to the stillness of classicism by recognizing that history advances only insofar as it is guided by those *eternal norms*, which the idea of stillness represents and which the modern world seems to have lost sight of.

Chapter 7

1. See Eykman.
2. Lothar Köhn's detailed study on attempts between 1918 and 1933 "jenseits der Historisierung zu einem neuen Absolutum vorzustoßen" (752) presupposes this insight.
3. See, above all, Broch's essayistic reflections in *Die Schlafwandler*. Benn's "Verlorenes Ich" is in certain respects not dissimilar; see *GW*, 3:215–16.
4. See Kaufmann, especially 4–18, 40–46, 78, 225–27, 284–306, and 417.
5. By focusing on the ideas that contributed to national socialism, I do not mean to minimize complementary accounts that focus on such matters as politics, economics, sociology, or even psychology. I am dealing here with merely one aspect of a highly complex configuration.
6. Cf. Nietzsche, *Werke*, 3:314 and 751.
7. Cf. ibid., 2:589 and 3:919.
8. Cf. ibid., 3:441.
9. Nietzsche's immediate tolerance exhibits itself in statements such as the following from *Also sprach Zarathustra*: " 'Das—ist nun *mein* Weg—wo ist der eure?' so antwortete ich denen, welche mich 'nach dem Wege' fragten. *Den Weg nämlich—den gibt es nicht!*" (emphasis in the original, *Werke*, 2:443). Cf. 2:697. The self-cancellation of this position is sometimes hinted at, but the consequences are never drawn; see 2:36 and 586.
10. Followers of Nietzsche—for example, Nehamas (see especially 36, 49, 72–73)—tend to separate perspectivism, the idea that no position can be ultimately grounded but that one can argue for the validity of one position over another, from relativism, the idea that all positions are equally valid. The distinction may be heuristically useful, but it is philosophically unsound. If, as in perspectivism, no position can be grounded, then my defense of a position leads to an infinite regress and is as such ultimately arbitrary and invalid; relativism is the consequence. If, as in relativism, all positions are equally valid, then I am of course free to assert the validity of my position at the expense of another. My exclusion of the other position is necessarily valid; relativism passes over into perspectivism. I use the terms, therefore, interchangeably.
11. Cf. Nietzsche, *Werke*, 3:424, as well as Zarathustra's encounters with the soothsayer and the shadow.
12. During his brief declaration for the national socialist regime, Benn, recognizing no absolute content, was willing to support those who would decide what is valid and what is invalid life. His essay "Geist und Seele künftiger Geschlechter" is at one with the tenets of what would eventually lead to the national socialist programs of forced sterilization and euthanasia.
13. My argument is not that history plays no role in the development or justification of norms, but that history alone cannot ground norms. It would be useful to recognize three levels of norms. First, some positions, such as the arbitrary advantage of the more powerful—evidenced, for example, in slavery—are categorically wrong; they are self-contradictory. The establish-

ment of norms against injustice follows from reason. Second, some norms, though not absolutely valid, are compatible with reason and can be viewed as necessary under specific historical conditions. For example, it is necessary that laws limiting the consumption of water be introduced in a society that has a restricted supply of usable water. Third, some norms cannot be deduced from reason or history; they are decisionistic. It does not matter what the norm is, merely that there be a norm—for example, whether one drives on the right or the left: either is appropriate, but in a particular culture it must be one or the other. Cf. Hegel, 7:34–46. Benn's mistake was in part his abandonment of rational and historical norms in favor of decisionistic stasis.

14. *Zur Genealogie der Moral* obviously lends support to such a comparison.

15. See Nietzsche, *Werke*, 3:557–58, and cf. 2:645–47.

16. The need for a defense of nonrelativism has not vanished despite the paradigmatic refutation of relativism by Socrates/Plato; this should be especially evident to students of literary criticism. See, most recently, Barbara Herrnstein Smith. Smith views her relativism, not as a claim or an argument, but rather as a style or taste; nonetheless, she does present arguments and does seek to avoid contradictions (183). Her position, despite its sophistication, strikes me as no less vulnerable than other forms of relativism. First, if, according to her own metaclaims, she cannot ground relativism or even assert the untenability of objectivism, then her objections to objectivism are self-erasing. Since objectivism is as tenable as relativism (despite Smith's personal preference for the latter), and since objectivism denies the truth of relativism, it follows that relativism is untenable. Second, if, as Smith argues (e.g., 151), there are no fixed truths, then it is only consequential that this very claim pass over into another claim—but not another relativistic claim, for that would mean the fixity, or absoluteness, of relativism; the self-reflexive truth of relativism is, rather, its own relativity.

17. Recognition of pragmatic contradictions is central to the transcendental pragmatics of Apel and Kuhlmann, as well as to the outstanding work on objective idealism being done by Hösle, Jermann, and Wandschneider.

18. Not all Nietzsche scholars are blind to this quandary. Consider, for example, the question Bernd Magnus raises: "If all theories are perspectives, is not the theory which states that all theories are perspectives also (merely) a perspective?" (196–97). Unfortunately, Magnus and others fail to pursue Nietzsche's claim to its logical conclusion, that is, to its own self-refutation. The critic who comes closest is Nehamas, who admits that "it is *possible* that some views are not interpretations" (66). However, the claim that there *may* be absolute truth is a contradiction in terms (it renders nonhypothetical truth hypothetical); the logically consistent position would assert that if absolute truth is possible, it is not only possible but necessary. An absolute position is either apodictically negative—i.e., impossible—or apodictically positive—i.e., necessary. Similarly, Nehamas admits that Nietzsche cannot, without contradicting himself, abandon unconditional values unconditionally (224)—yet conditional unconditional values are again contradictory. For a fuller discussion of the absolute with reference to both the Münchhausen trilemma and the question of modality see Hösle's essay on "Begründungsfragen."

19. It is in the structure of negative metaphysical propositions that when they become self-reflexive, they cancel themselves. Positive propositions do not suffer the same incoherence (this is succinctly illustrated in the self-reflexive consequences of the statement "This sentence is true" versus the proposition "This sentence is false"). Moreover, what appears circular in a positive metaphysical assertion is often transcendental, that is, universally necessary, thus presuppositionless and, therefore, not circular. The point is missed in R. H. Grimm's discussion of self-referentiality.

20. For a fuller discussion, with bibliographical references, see Roche, "Plato."

21. Plato, *Republic*, 361a.

22. It almost goes without saying that my critique of Nietzsche's metaphysical and epistemological framework does not erase the validity of certain individual insights. Systematic regress and material progress are in practice compatible. Nietzsche's cultural criticism, his psychological perceptions, and the rhetorical force of his arguments should not be underestimated, even as one attempts to counter his metatheoretical stance.

23. It is an unphilosophic practice to measure the validity of an idea by its genesis or consequences; it is, by the way, a particularly Nietzschean technique: see especially *Zur Genealogie der Moral*, also 2:596–98 and 3:779. Rosenberg follows Nietzsche in both respects.

24. The philosophical argument suggesting the passage from relativism to arbitrary absolutism has a psychological corollary, namely the decisionistic desire for stabilization, which may help explain Benn's initial infatuation with nazism. In this direction cf. Schröder, *Benn. Poesie*.

25. The most recent account of Rosenberg is Nova, who justly includes a chapter on Rosenberg's "Nonuniversalism" (169–78). However, Nova does not delve into the philosophical import of Rosenberg's nonuniversalism, and he states: "Any objective, logical refutation of the *Myth* is impossible" (xv). Such a position not only fails to counter Rosenberg, it confirms, as we will see, the metaposition from which Rosenberg derives the legitimacy of his own claims.

26. Attacks on reason and universal truth were widespread in other national socialist philosophers as well. See, for example, Heyse, 250–51 and 306–7; Beck, *Im Kampf*, 34–39 and 45–49; Beck, *Deutsche Vollendung*, 65–71, 509–13, 527, and 574–76; Bergmann, 7–15; Krieck, 1:37–38, 2:7–10, 3:7–20, and 3:123–31; and Böhm, 12–56. If Rauschning is to be believed, not only other philosophers, but Hitler himself shared Rosenberg's relativism. Hitler is reported to have said: "Es gibt keine Wahrheit, weder im moralischen noch wissenschaftlichen Sinne. Der Gedanke einer freien, voraussetzungslosen Wissenschaft konnte nur im Zeitalter des Liberalismus auftauchen. Er ist absurd" (Rauschning, 210).

27. Cf. Rosenberg, *Mythus*, 79 and 289.

28. See Hegel, 5:44. For why the assertion is well grounded see Wandschneider, "Absolutheit."

29. See Moeller van den Bruck (especially 311 and 323) for a similar denial of the universal, followed by the claim that because each nation necessarily

fails to understand and respect the next, it is free to fight for itself at the expense of others.

30. Nature is to be understood in this context as the negation of what, in philosophy and law, is called "natural right." For an incisive analysis of *natural* right as a misnomer see Hegel, 10:311–12.

31. See especially "Antwort an die literarischen Emigranten" (*GW*, 4:239–48).

32. Whisker discusses Nietzsche's impact on Rosenberg but fails to treat the important theme of relativism. Instead, he focuses on Nietzsche's attacks on Christianity and Christian ethics, the concept of will to power, the overman, and the philosopher's evaluation of war and heroism (14–31).

33. In an unfortunately long-forgotten document of the German exile, which is also one of the earliest and most prophetic, Helmuth Plessner draws similar consequences, suggesting that after the abjuration of reason, the most radical and consistent counterposition is the elevation of nature (or race) and mere power; see especially 16–17, 88, 131–41, and 179–82. The concern with universals, which many consider a characteristic element of inner emigration, was not restricted to the authors writing in Germany against national socialism. In this context one might also consider Oderbruck's prominent reference to "das Ewige Recht" in Zuckmayer, *Des Teufels General*, 153.

34. Cf. Rosenberg, *Mythus*, 119.

35. Cf. the position of Friedrich Alfred Beck and Josef Wagner in the "Hochschule für Politik der NSDAP": "Nationalsozialismus ist keine theoretische Idee, sondern eine biologische und geistige Grundlehre, eine Lebenstatsache und Lebensaufgabe von unmittelbarer, nicht weiter erklärbarer, sondern zu verwirklichender unerbittlicher Notwendigkeit. Nationalsozialismus ist keines Beweises fähig und bedarf keines Beweises" (Poliakov and Wulf, 45).

36. See the influential studies by Jellinek and Kelsen.

37. For further analysis see Hösle and Vitzthum.

38. The Basic Law of the Federal Republic of Germany avoids this self-canceling structure with its declaration that the elimination of articles 1 and 20 is inadmissible: see Art. 79, par. 3. This represents an advance over Weimar, and also over the U.S. Constitution, which in principle allows for the cancellation of its most basic, noncontingent points (even if such changes depend on state, rather than merely congressional, approval).

39. While not directly referring to the constitution, Benn nonetheless recognized in 1933, even as he sided with the movement, that national socialism was directed "gegen eine Gesellschaft, die überhaupt keine Maßstäbe mehr schafft, kein transzendentes Recht mehr errichtet" (*GW*, 1:444). Such a society, according to Benn, loses its right to exist; it gets what it deserves: "und verdient denn eine solche Gesellschaft etwas anderes als Joch und neues Gesetz?" (ibid.).

40. Recent attempts to overcome the so-called false dichotomy between objectivism and relativism—as, for example, in Bernstein, Kolb, and Margolis—are, I believe, less persuasive than other accounts, such as those of

Kuhlmann and Hösle, that argue for first principles. However, to go into this matter in further detail would be to write another book, one only remotely related to Benn. My point in this chapter is simply that Benn was correct to strive for an absolute, for stasis, though his methods, as I will attempt to show in the next chapter, were inappropriate to his task.

41. Since a valid absolute philosophy asserts itself not directly but rather by exhibiting contradictions in alternative positions, such a philosophy is tolerant in a truer sense than is a perspectival one, for it is willing to weigh counterpositions; it takes their claims to truth seriously and recognizes only immanent critique.

42. It is perhaps not irrelevant to mention in this context that the resistance movement against Hitler was in part informed by the categories of transcendental idealism. One thinks of Adam von Trott zu Solz, a member of the Stauffenberg circle, whose dissertation of 1932 explored international justice from the perspective of Hegel's *Philosophie des Rechts*; or of Hans Scholl and Kurt Huber, central figures in the resistance group known as "The White Rose"—the former was a careful reader of Plato, the latter a consequent Kantian. See Scholl, 21, and Leber, 44–46.

43. Already Socrates argues in the *Euthydemus* that the lack of objective norms leads not only to skepticism but beyond skepticism to subjectivism: "no one speaks falsely" (286e). Cf. *Theaetetus*, 161b–e.

Chapter 8

1. My critique of Benn not only draws on the poems discussed above but also considers his essayistic reflections insofar as they shed light on the concept *Statik*. Not every point of critique will apply directly to the poems. Willems has, I think, done a great service for future Benn criticism by cogently arguing that there is far more wisdom in Benn's poetry than in his theoretical reflections; see Willems 28–52.

2. The student of German literature will recognize a connection here to Thomas Mann, specifically his reflections on music and German history in *Doktor Faustus*.

3. Cf. Steinhagen, "Gottfried Benn 1933," 41–44.

4. Also in this direction see Stollmann, "Gottfried Benn," especially 292 and 294–95.

5. See Wandschneider, "Die dialektische Notwendigkeit."

6. It is in this context no coincidence that national socialism gave little weight to substantive primary virtues such as goodness or justice, but rather worked with the secondary virtues of loyalty, courage, self-sacrifice, etc.

7. See especially Petzold, but also, to an extent, Fritz Stern, *Politics*, 183–266.

8. The general proximity of Benn to Heidegger is implied in Hillebrand's clear but uncritical treatment of both thinkers.

9. The passage stems from Hitler's closing address: "Das deutsche Volk ist

glücklich in dem Bewußtsein, daß die ewige Flut der Erscheinungen nun mehr endgültig abgelöst wurde von einem ruhenden Pol" (*Der Triumph des Willens*).

10. The phrase, which stems from Walter Benjamin (I, 2:469), has been given material substance in Stollmann, *Ästhetisierung der Politik*.

11. Most interpreters of Benn find his association with nazism an aberration. In some senses it is, but in others, his affirmation of the movement appears to have been, if not necessary, at least consequential. Cf. Wellershoff, 155–97.

12. This is not to deny an abstract content of nationalism and militarism—i.e., a content informed by the formal virtues of loyalty and courage—nor is it to dispute the existence of a submerged content informed by injustice.

13. The one thematically significant difference is the national socialist elevation of will, action, and effect as opposed to Benn's elevation of indifference and withdrawal. Whether the two structures collapse politically will be addressed below.

14. An obvious difference between Benn and the sonnet writers of the inner emigration is that Benn embraces less a conventional than an innovative and unique concept of form.

15. Jungrichter, *Ideologie und Tradition: Studien zur nationalsozialistischen Sonettdichtung*.

16. Carl Schmitt is the most notable example. The idea is also visible in Nazi poetry; for example, in Heinrich Anacker, "'Hitler, der Fels im Chaos'" (13), or Will Vesper, "Der Grundstein" (in Kober, 12–13).

17. Cf. *Oelze* no. 2 (27 January 1933).

18. The different aims of Benn and perspectival painters (or even the weighty differences between Uccello, Piranesi, and Escher) do not argue against this point. The absolutization of form lends itself, in its association with subjectivity, to diverse purposes.

19. I do not mean here or elsewhere to reduce Benn's poetry to this moment. Nonetheless, the search for an absolute is central, and it is closely intertwined with the poet's elevation of stasis.

20. Propositions such as those above may strike the contemporary reader as anachronistic, perhaps even naive. I have tried, however, in my excursus on transcendental norms, to argue that the law of noncontradiction is the only tenable standard on which to base ethical norms. The reader familiar with recent discussions in Germany on reflexive foundationalism, as evidenced in the excellent work by Apel, Kuhlmann, and Hösle, will not find my position quite so surprising.

21. In this respect Benn differs from most writers of the inner emigration, a large number of whom embrace a Christian world view. One thinks of Bergengruen, Schneider, Schröder, Haushofer, and others. Cf. especially Baden and Klieneberger, but also Hoffmann, *Opposition Poetry*.

22. Weber, *Gottfried Benn: Zwischen Christentum und Gnosis*.

23. For an excellent unmasking of what Heidegger would call *Gerede*, see GW, 3:294. Cf. GW, 3:299.

24. See *GW*, 1:577, 2:151, 2:224, and 3:296; *Oelze* no. 88 (28 July 1936) and no. 308 (27 May 1946). The self-cancellation of the monologue poem is not unrelated to Mallarmé's paradoxical reflections in his "Crise de vers"; see especially 363–64 and 366–67.

25. In addition, Benn's claim that unintelligible art is no more alienating than injustice, senseless war, or the blind accumulation of power can hardly be viewed as a legitimate argument for unintelligible art; see *GW*, 1:314.

26. Cf. Ryan, 25–26.

27. *GW*, 3:331. For Benn, the gods' silence is a recurring topos; see especially *GW*, 3:104, 113, and 464.

28. Hegel is helpful in deciphering this structure: "Das Sein reduziert sich somit von selbst auf das bloße *Außer mir*, und es soll auch ausdrücklich nur das *Negative meiner* bedeuten, in welcher Negation in der Tat mir nichts übrigbleibt als Ich selbst,—es heißt leeres Stroh dreschen, jenes Negative meiner, das Außer oder Über mir, für eine behauptete oder wenigstens geglaubte, anerkannte Objektivität ausgeben zu wollen, denn es ist damit nur ein *Negatives* ausgesprochen, und zwar ausdrücklich durch mich" (emphasis in the original, 16:348–49). Cf. 12:27, 16:180–83, and 18:168.

29. It would be interesting to reflect on whether it was partly Benn's monologic disregard for reception aesthetics that led him to affirm poetic form and closure as in principle static and final, whereas for most of modernity poetic closure is a contradiction in terms.

30. This structure is also implicit in Benn's later concept of "das sich umgrenzende Ich." The limit functions from both sides: each side has its being by virtue of the limit, by virtue of its not being other, yet the limit is common to both; it connects as well as separates. On the dialectical structure of the category "Grenze" see Hegel, 5:131–39.

31. See especially Seneca, *De tranquillitate animi*, 3:1–8; 4:1–8; 17:3.

32. See especially letter no. 9, and *De tranquillitate animi*, 7:1–4; also the following passage from letter no. 48: "You should live for the other person if you wish to live for yourself" ["alteri vivas oportet, si vis tibi vivere"].

33. See Roche, *Dynamic Stillness*, 163–71.

34. See especially "Das moderne Ich" (*GW*, 1:7–22) and "Verlorenes Ich" (*GW*, 3:215–16).

35. See especially "Wer allein ist—." On the relevance of this distinction see Roche, "Plato."

36. In particular, Hölderlin's *Hyperion* and the late hymns—for example, "Der Rhein" (2:142–48).

37. Benn's stance vis-à-vis totality is contradictory. He often embraces it in his poetic works but then separates an intellectual totality from the otherness of reality, thus undermining the concept of totality. At times he explicitly censures the drive for totality and synthesis; see, for example, *GW*, 2:212 and 4:164.

38. In addition, the poet's position is not as stable as the poet would like, for the majority position inevitably shifts with time.

39. Cf. Roche, *Dynamic Stillness*, 178–244, especially 187.

40. See also *B*, 61.

41. Cf. Apel, who sees from this perspective not a contradiction, but a complementarity, between scientific objectivity (or analytic philosophy) and moral subjectivity (or existentialism). Benn appears to have captured this position in both a poetic and a representative way. For a clear expository expression of this dualism see *Oelze* no. 2 (27 January 1933).

42. Cf. Apel, especially 359.

Chapter 9

1. For this reason I would disagree with Jochen Schulte-Sasse's claim, which he shares with numerous practitioners (see, for example, Schnell, *Literarische Innere Emigration*, 55), that critics should focus on the historical conditions of a work (see especially 62 and 70–72). Though such an enterprise is legitimate (my own discussion of "*Statik* and Inner Emigration" presupposes its validity), it is not an enterprise that reveals the value of the artwork as art, and it should not, therefore, be viewed as the essence of literary criticism.

2. By using the term *aesthetic* in the setting of an explicitly objective-idealist framework, I hope to avoid any confusion with the use of *aesthetic* as that which is merely formal.

3. A classic illustration of this point would be Rāmacandra's *Rasikarañjana*, a Sanskrit text from 1524: read one way it is an ascetic work; read another way it is an erotic work. The reader is not free to choose one reading or the other; the work reveals in its formal dimensions the speculative unity of the ascetic and the erotic, a unity familiar within the Christian tradition as well. Cf. Winternitz, 3:150–51.

4. One might want to counter this criticism by suggesting that all positions are contradictory and that the demonstration of a contradiction says nothing about the truth value of a particular stance. With Nietzsche and his modern adherents, one could then claim that contradictions are to be endured or embraced, not overcome. Such a stance, however, is untenable. If one substitutes, self-reflexively, for each a in the expression $a \wedge \text{non-}a$ the entire expression $a \wedge \text{non-}a$, then the result is the negation of $a \wedge \text{non-}a$—that is, the truth of the statement that contradictions are to be endured is its own falsity: $(a \wedge \text{non-}a) \wedge \text{non-}(a \wedge \text{non-}a)$. See Hösle, *Wahrheit und Geschichte*, 282.

5. The critique applies, for example, to Jochen Schulte-Sasse, whose position was cited above in another context.

Works Cited

Primary Sources

Works by Gottfried Benn

B *Ausgewählte Briefe*. Wiesbaden: Limes, 1957.
DD *Gottfried Benn. Dichter über ihre Dichtungen*. Edited by Edgar Lohner. Wiesbaden: Limes, n.d.
GW *Gesammelte Werke in vier Bänden*. Edited by Dieter Wellershoff. Wiesbaden: Limes, 1958–61.
H *Briefwechsel mit Paul Hindemith*. Edited by Ann Clark Fehn. Wiesbaden: Limes, 1978.
Oelze *Briefe an F. W. Oelze*. Edited by Harald Steinhagen and Jürgen Schröder. 2 vols. Wiesbaden: Limes, 1977–80.
R *Gottfried Benn: The Unreconstructed Expressionist*. Edited by J. M. Ritchie. Modern German Authors. Texts and Contexts 6. London: Wolff, 1972.
S *Prose, Essays, Poems*. Edited by Volkmar Sander. The German Library 73. New York: Continuum, 1987.
SP *Selected Poems*. Edited by Friedrich Wilhelm Wodtke. Oxford: Oxford University Press, 1970.
SW *Sämtliche Werke. Stuttgarter Ausgabe*. Edited by Gerhard Schuster. 3 vols. to date. Stuttgart: Klett-Cotta, 1986–.
T *Den Traum alleine tragen. Neue Texte, Briefe, Dokumente*. Edited by Paul Raabe and Max Niedermayer. 2nd ed. Munich: Deutscher Taschenbuch Verlag, 1975.

Works by Other Authors

Anacker, Heinrich. *Die Trommel: S.A. = Gedichte*. 3rd ed. Munich: Eher, 1935.
Aristotle. *The Basic Works of Aristotle*. Edited by Richard McKeon. New York: Random House, 1941.
Arnold, Heinz Ludwig, ed. *Deutsche Literatur im Exil 1933–1945*. 2 vols. Frankfurt am Main: Athenäum, 1974.
Beck, Friedrich Alfred. *Deutsche Vollendung: Idee und Wirklichkeit des nationalsozialistischen Reiches*. 2nd ed. Posen: Feldmüller, 1944.
———. *Im Kampf um die Philosophie des lebendigen Geistes: Ein Aufruf in zehn Thesen*. Breslau: Hirt, 1936.
Bergmann, Ernst. *Die natürliche Geistlehre: System einer deutsch-nordischen Weltsinndeutung*. Stuttgart: Truckenmüller, 1937.
Die Bibel oder die ganze Heilige Schrift des Alten und Neuen Testaments nach der Übersetzung Martin Luthers. Stuttgart: Württembergische Bibelanstalt, 1970.

Böhm, Franz. *Anti-Cartesianismus: Deutsche Philosophie im Widerstand.* Leipzig: Meiner, 1938.
Böhme, Herbert, ed. *Rufe in das Reich: Die heldische Dichtung von Langemarck bis zur Gegenwart.* Berlin: Junge Generation, 1934.
Bonaventure, Saint. *Itinerarium Mentis in Deum.* In his *Opera Omnia,* 12:1–21. Paris, 1868.
Brecht, Bertolt. *Gesammelte Werke in 20 Bänden.* Frankfurt: Suhrkamp, 1967.
Diels, Hermann, and Walther Kranz, eds. *Die Fragmente der Vorsokratiker.* 6th ed. Vol 1. Berlin: Weidemann, 1951.
Diettrich, Fritz. *Werke.* Edited by Wilfried Brennecke. 3 vols. Göttingen: Sachse, 1963–66.
Droste-Hülshoff, Annette von. *Gedichte.* Edited by Siegfried Sudhof. Stuttgart: Reclam, 1974.
Eckermann, Johann Peter. *Gespräche mit Goethe in den letzten Jahren seines Lebens.* Edited by Ernst Beutler. Munich: Deutscher Taschenbuch Verlag, 1976.
Eckhart, Meister. *Die deutschen und lateinischen Werke.* Hrsg. im Auftrage der deutschen Forschungsgemeinschaft. Stuttgart: Kohlhammer, 1936–. (abbreviated as *DW* and *LW*)
Eichendorff, Joseph von. *Gedichte. Eine Auswahl.* Stuttgart: Reclam, 1966.
Fichte, Johann Gottlieb. *Johann Gottlieb Fichtes sämmtliche Werke.* Edited by I. H. Fichte. 8 vols. Berlin: Veit, 1845–46.
Goethe, Johann Wolfgang von. *Goethes Werke.* Edited by Erich Trunz. 10th ed. 14 vols. Munich: Beck, 1974.
Gryphius, Andreas. *Catharina von Georgien. Trauerspiel.* Edited by Alois M. Haas. Stuttgart: Reclam, 1975.
———. *Großmütiger Rechtsgelehrter oder Sterbender Aemilius Paulus Papinianus.* Edited by Ilse-Marie Barth. Stuttgart: Reclam, 1968.
Hagelstange, Rudolf. "Die Form als erste Entscheidung." In *Mein Gedicht ist mein Messer: Lyriker zu ihren Gedichten,* edited by Hans Bender, 35–41. Heidelberg: Rothe, 1955.
———. *Venezianisches Credo.* Munich: List, 1975.
Härtle, Heinrich, ed. *Großdeutschland: Traum und Tragödie. Rosenbergs Kritik am Hitlerismus.* 2nd ed. Munich: Härtle, 1970.
Hegel, G. W. F. *Werke in zwanzig Bänden.* Edited by Eva Moldenhauer and Karl Markus Michel. Frankfurt am Main: Suhrkamp, 1970.
Heidegger, Martin. *Sein und Zeit.* 7th ed. Tübingen: Niemeyer, 1953.
Heine, Heinrich. *Sämtliche Schriften.* Edited by Klaus Briegleb et al. 6 vols. Munich: Hanser, 1968–76.
Herder, Johann Gottfried von. *Herders sämmtliche Werke.* Edited by Bernhard Suphan. 32 vols. Berlin: Weidmann, 1877–1913.
Heyse, Hans. *Idee und Existenz.* Hamburg: Hanseatische Verlagsanstalt, 1935.
Hölderlin, Christian Friedrich. *Sämtliche Werke. Große Stuttgarter Ausgabe.* Edited by Friedrich Beißner. 8 vols. Stuttgart: Kohlhammer, 1946–85.
Jellinek, Georg. *Allgemeine Staatslehre.* 3rd ed. Berlin: Springer, 1922.
Jünger, Friedrich Georg. *Sämtliche Gedichte.* Edited by Citta Jünger. 2 vols. Stuttgart: Klett-Cotta, 1985.

Kant, Immanuel. *Werke in zwanzig Bänden*. Edited by Wilhelm Weischedel. Frankfurt am Main: Suhrkamp, 1968.
Kelsen, Hans. *Allgemeine Staatslehre*. Berlin: Springer, 1925.
Kober, Julius. *Vortragsbuch für Front und Heimat: Erlesene Perlen ernster und heiterer Dichtung aus zwei Jahrhunderten mit Anleitung für die Vortragskunst und die Programmgestaltung*. Gotha: Engelhard-Reyher, 1942.
Krieck, Ernst. *Völkisch = politische Anthropologie*. 3 vols. 2nd ed. Leipzig: Armanen = Verlag, 1938.
Langenbucher, Hellmuth. *Die deutsche Gegenwartsdichtung: Eine Einführung in das volkhafte Schrifttum unserer Zeit*. Berlin: Junker, 1940.
Lao-tzu. *Tao Te Ching*. Translated by Stephen Mitchell. New York: Harper and Row, 1988.
Leber, Annedore. *Das Gewissen steht auf. 64 Lebensbilder aus dem deutschen Widerstand 1933–1945*. Edited by Willy Brandt and Karl Dietrich Bracher. Berlin: Mosaik, 1954.
Leip, Hans. *Kadenzen: Neue Gedichte*. Stuttgart: Cotta, 1942.
Liederbuch der Nationalsozialistischen Deutschen Arbeiterpartei. 52nd ed. Munich: Eher, 1941.
Lipsius, Justus. *Opera Omnia*. 4 vols. Wesel, 1675.
Lucretius. *De rerum natura*. The Loeb Classical Library. Cambridge: Harvard University Press; London: Heinemann, 1975.
Mallarmé, Stéphane. *Oeuvres Complètes*. Edited by Henri Mondor and G. Jean-Aubry. Paris: Pléiade, 1945.
May, Herbert, and Bruce Metzger, eds. *The New Oxford Annotated Bible with the Apocrypha. Revised Standard Version*. New York: Oxford University Press, 1973.
Meyer, Semi. *Die Geistige Wirklichkeit: Der Geist im Gefüge der Welt*. Stuttgart: Enke, 1925.
Moeller van den Bruck, Arthur. *Das dritte Reich*. Edited by Hans Schwarz. 3rd ed. Hamburg: Hanseatische Verlagsanstalt, 1931.
Mörike, Eduard. *Gedichte. Eine Auswahl*. Edited by Erwin Ackerknecht. Stuttgart: Reclam, 1975.
Nemerov, Howard. *The Collected Poems of Howard Nemerov*. Chicago and London: The University of Chicago Press, 1977.
Nietzsche, Friedrich. "Vereinsamt." In *Deutsche Gedichte. Von den Anfängen bis zur Gegenwart*, edited by Theodor Echtemeyer and Benno von Wiese, 514–15. Düsseldorf: Bagel, 1956.
―――. *Werke*. Edited by Karl Schlechta. 6th ed. 3 vols. Munich: Hanser, 1969.
Opitz, Martin. "Lob des Feldtlebens." In *Weltliche Poemata 1644. Erster Teil*, edited by Erich Trunz, 233–44. Deutsche Neudrucke. Barock 2. Tübingen: Niemeyer, 1967.
―――. "Sta Viator!" In *Deutsche Dichtung des Barock*, edited by Edgar Hederer, 16. 3rd ed. Munich: Hanser, 1961.
Plato. *The Collected Dialogues including the Letters*. Edited by Edith Hamilton and Huntington Cairns. Bollingen Series 71. Princeton: Princeton University Press, 1978.

Plessner, Helmuth. *Das Schicksal deutschen Geistes im Ausgang seiner bürgerlichen Epoche*. Zurich: Niehans, 1935.
Poliakov, Leon, and Joseph Wulf, eds. *Das Dritte Reich und seine Denker*. Munich: Saur, 1978.
Rauschning, Hermann. *Gespräche mit Hitler*. New York: Europa, 1940.
Richter, Johann Paul Friedrich [Jean Paul]. *Werke*. 6 vols. Munich: Hanser, 1959–73.
Rilke, Rainer Maria. "Archaïscher Torso Apollos." In *Deutsche Gedichte. Von den Anfängen bis zur Gegenwart*, edited by Theodor Echtemeyer and Benno von Wiese, 468. Düsseldorf: Bagel, 1956.
———. *Die Aufzeichnungen des Malte Laurids Brigge*. Bibliothek Suhrkamp 343. Frankfurt am Main: Suhrkamp, 1975.
Rimbaud. *Oeuvres*. Paris: Garnier Frères, 1960.
Rohde, Erwin. *Psyche: Seelencult und Unsterblichkeitsglaube der Griechen*. 2 vols. 1894. Darmstadt: Wissenschaftliche Buchgesellschaft, 1980.
Rosenberg, Alfred. *Letzte Aufzeichnungen: Ideale und Idole der nationalsozialistischen Revolution*. Göttingen: Plesse, 1955.
———. *Der Mythus des 20. Jahrhunderts: Eine Wertung der seelisch-geistigen Gestaltenkämpfe unserer Zeit*. Munich: Hoheneichen, 1943.
Schiller, Friedrich. *Gedichte. Eine Auswahl*. Edited by Gerhard Fricke. Stuttgart: Reclam, 1978.
———. *Schillers Werke. Nationalausgabe*. Edited by Julius Peterson and Hermann Schneider. Weimar: Böhlaus, 1943–.
Schopenhauer, Arthur. *Zürcher Ausgabe in zehn Bänden*. Zurich: Diogenes, 1977.
Seneca. *Ad Lucilium Epistolae Morales*. 3 vols. The Loeb Classical Library. Cambridge: Harvard University Press; London: Heinemann, 1953.
———. *Letters from a Stoic*. Edited and translated by Robin Campbell. New York: Penguin, 1969.
Shaftesbury, Anthony, Earl of. *Characteristics of Men, Manners, Opinions, Times*. Edited by John M. Robertson. 2 vols. London: Richards, 1900.
Silesius, Angelus [Johannes Scheffler]. *Cherubinischer Wandersmann. Kritische Ausgabe*. Edited by Louise Gnädinger. Stuttgart: Reclam, 1984.
Spengler, Oswald. *Der Untergang des Abendlandes. Umrisse einer Morphologie der Weltgeschichte*. 7th ed. Munich: Deutscher Taschenbuch Verlag, 1983.
Stifter, Adalbert. *Brigitta*. Stuttgart: Reclam, 1978.
———. *Der Nachsommer*. Munich: Deutscher Taschenbuch Verlag, 1977.
Suso, Heinrich. *Deutsche Schriften*. Edited by Karl Bihlmeyer. Stuttgart: Kohlhammer, 1907.
Tauler, Johannes. *Die Predigten Taulers aus der Engelberger und der Freiburger Handschrift sowie aus Schmidts Abschriften der ehemaligen Straßburger Handschriften*. Edited by Ferdinand Vetter. Deutsche Texte des Mittelalters 11. Berlin: Weidmann, 1910.
Der Triumph des Willens: Das Dokument vom Reichsparteitag 1934. Directed by Leni Riefenstahl. NSDAP, 1936.
Wiechert, Ernst. *Sämtliche Werke in zehn Bänden*. Vienna: Desch, 1957.

Winckelmann, Johann Joachim. *Gedanken über die Nachahmung der griechischen Werke in der Malerei und Bildhauerkunst.* Edited by Ludwig Uhlig. Stuttgart: Reclam, 1977.
Zuckmayer, Carl. *Des Teufels General. Drama in drei Akten.* Frankfurt am Main: Fischer, 1973.

Secondary Sources

Allemann, Beda. *Gottfried Benn. Das Problem der Geschichte.* Pfullingen: Neske, 1963.
Alter, Reinhard. *Gottfried Benn. The Artist and Politics (1910–1934).* Bern: Lang, 1976.
———. "Gottfried Benn und Börries von Münchhausen. Ein Briefwechsel aus den Jahren 1933/34." *Jahrbuch der deutschen Schillergesellschaft* 25 (1981): 139–70.
Apel, Karl-Otto. "Das Apriori der Kommunikationsgemeinschaft und die Grundlagen der Ethik." In his *Transformation der Philosophie,* 2:358–435. Frankfurt am Main: Suhrkamp, 1976.
Baden, Hans Jürgen. "Wort im Widerstand—die protestantische Dichtung im Dritten Reich." In his *Poesie und Theologie,* 177–203. Hamburg: Agentur des Rauhen Hauses, 1971.
Baird, Jay W. "From Berlin to Neubabelsberg: Nazi Film Propaganda and Hitler Youth Quex." *Journal of Contemporary History* 18 (1983): 495–515.
Baumgärtner, Raimund. *Weltanschauungskampf im Dritten Reich: Die Auseinandersetzung der Kirchen mit Rosenberg.* Mainz: Grünewald, 1977.
Bayerdörfer, Hans-Peter. "Weimarer Republik." In *Geschichte der deutschen Lyrik von Mittelalter bis zur Gegenwart,* edited by Walter Hinderer, 439–76. Stuttgart: Reclam, 1983.
Belgum, Kirsten, Karoline Kirst-Gundersen, and Paul Levesque. " 'Faust im Braunhemd': Germanistik and Fascism." In *Our 'Faust'? Roots and Ramifactions of a Modern German Myth,* edited by Reinhold Grimm and Jost Hermand, 153–67. Madison: University of Wisconsin Press, 1987.
Benjamin, Walter. *Gesammelte Schriften.* Edited by Rolf Tiedemann and Hermann Schweppenhäuser. 6 vols. Frankfurt am Main: Suhrkamp, 1972–85.
Berning, Cornelia. "Die Sprache des Nationalsozialismus." *Zeitschrift für die Wortforschung* 16 (1960): 71–118, 178–88; 17 (1961): 83–121, 171–82; 18 (1962): 108–18, 160–72; 19 (1963): 92–112.
Bernstein, Richard J. *Beyond Objectivism and Relativism: Science, Hermeneutics, and Praxis.* Philadelphia: University of Pennsylvania Press, 1983.
Bielefeld, Michael. "Bestätigung tiefster Zerrüttung: Zum Reise-Motiv und seiner Bedeutung bei Gottfried Benn." In *Gottfried Benn,* edited by Heinz Ludwig Arnold, 54–62. 2nd ed. Text und Kritik 44. Munich: Text und Kritik, 1985.
Bormann, Alexander von. "Das nationalsozialistische Gemeinschaftslied." In *Die deutsche Literatur im Dritten Reich: Themen—Traditionen—Wirkungen,*

edited by Horst Denkler and Karl Prümm, 256–80. Stuttgart: Reclam, 1976.

Brackert, Helmut. "Nicht mehr Stirb und nicht mehr Werde. Zu Gottfried Benns Goethe-Bild." In *Festgabe für Ulrich Pretzel*, edited by Werner Simon, Wolfgang Bachofer, and Wolfgang Dittmann, 289–300. Berlin: Schmidt, 1963.

Brekle, Wolfgang. *Schriftsteller im antifaschistischen Widerstand 1933–1945 in Deutschland*. Berlin: Aufbau, 1985.

Brode, Hanspeter. "Studien zu Gottfried Benn. I. Mythologie, Naturwissenschaft und Geschichtsphilosophie. Café- und Inselmotive, Gehirnbeschreibung und Kulturkreislehre bei Benn." *Deutsche Vierteljahrsschrift für Literaturwissenschaft und Geistesgeschichte* 46 (1972): 714–63.

———. "Studien zu Gottfried Benn. II. Anspielung und Zitat als sinngebende Elemente moderner Lyrik. Benns Gedicht 'Widmung.' " *Deutsche Vierteljahrsschrift für Literaturwissenschaft und Geistesgeschichte* 47 (1973): 286–309.

Casper, M. Kent. "The Circle and the Centre: Symbols of Totality in Gottfried Benn." *German Life and Letters* 26 (1972–73): 288–97.

Chick, Edson M. "Ernst Wiechert's Flight to the Circle of Eternity." *Germanic Review* 30 (1955): 282–93.

De Mendelssohn, Peter. *Der Geist in der Despotie: Versuche über die moralischen Möglichkeiten des Intellektuellen in der totalitären Gesellschaft*. Berlin-Grunewald: Herbig, 1953.

Eykman, Christoph. "Der Verlust des Absoluten: Die geistesgeschichtliche Deutung des Nationalsozialismus in den Schriften der Exilautoren." In *Deutschsprachige Exilliteratur: Studien zu ihrer Bestimmung im Kontext der Epoche 1930 bis 1960*, edited by Wulf Koepke and Michael Winkler, 204–14. Studien zur Literatur der Moderne 12. Bonn: Bouvier, 1984.

Fick, Joseph. "Gottfried Benn: 'Reisen.' " In *Interpretationen moderner Lyrik*, edited by Otmar Bohusch, 86–89. Frankfurt am Main: Diesterweg, 1954.

Fischer, Bernhard. " 'Stil' und 'Züchtung'—Gottfried Benns Kunsttheorie und das Jahr 1933." *Internationales Archiv für Sozialgeschichte der deutschen Literatur* 12 (1987): 190–212.

Fredsted, Elin. "Die politische Lyrik des deutschen Faschismus." *Text und Kontext* 8 (1980): 353–77.

Friedrich, Hugo. *Die Struktur der modernen Lyrik*. 2nd ed. Hamburg: Rowohlt, 1967.

Gamm, Hans-Jochen. *Der braune Kult: Das Dritte Reich und seine Ersatzreligion. Ein Beitrag zur politischen Bildung*. Hamburg: Rütter, 1962.

Geißler, Rolf. "Dichter und Dichtung des Nationalsozialismus." In *Handbuch der deutschen Gegenwartsliteratur*, edited by Herbert Wiesner, 2:409–18. 2nd ed. Munich: Nymphenburger Verlagshandlung, 1969–70.

Gerth, Klaus. "Absolute Dichtung? Zu einem Begriff in der Poetik Gottfried Benns." In *Gottfried Benn*, edited by Bruno Hillebrand, 240–60. Wege der Forschung 316. Darmstadt: Wissenschaftliche Buchgesellschaft, 1979.

Grimm, Reinhold. *Gottfried Benn. Die farbliche Chiffre in der Dichtung*. 2nd ed.

Erlanger Beiträge zur Sprach- und Kunstwissenschaft. Nuremberg: Carl, 1962.

———. "Im Dickicht der inneren Emigration." In *Die deutsche Literatur im Dritten Reich: Themen—Traditionen—Wirkungen*, edited by Horst Denkler and Karl Prümm, 406–26. Stuttgart: Reclam, 1976.

Grimm, Rüdiger Hermann. "Circularity and Self-Reference in Nietzsche." *Metaphilosophy* 10 (1979): 289–305.

Hartung, Günter. *Literatur und Ästhetik des deutschen Faschismus: Drei Studien.* Berlin: Akademie-Verlag, 1983.

Heimann, Bodo. "Ich-Zerfall als Thema und Stil. Untersuchung zur dichterischen Sprache Gottfried Benns." *Germanisch-Romanische Monatsschrift* 14 (1964): 384–403.

Hillebrand, Bruno. *Artistik und Auftrag. Zur Kunsttheorie von Benn und Nietzsche.* Munich: Nymphenburg, 1966.

Hoffmann, Charles W. *Opposition Poetry in Nazi Germany.* University of California Publications in Modern Philology 67. Berkeley: University of California Press, 1962.

———. "Opposition und innere Emigration: Zwei Aspekte des 'Anderen Deutschlands.'" In *Exil und innere Emigration II*, edited by Peter Uwe Hohendahl and Egon Schwarz, 119–40. Internationale Tagung in St. Louis. Frankfurt am Main: Athenäum, 1973.

Homeyer, Helene. "Gottfried Benn und die Antike." *Zeitschrift für deutsche Philologie* 79 (1960): 113–24.

Hösle, Vittorio. "Begründungsfragen des objektiven Idealismus." In *Begründung und Philosophie*, edited by Forum für Philosophie Bad Homburg, 212–67. Frankfurt am Main: Suhrkamp, 1987.

———. "Carl Schmitts Kritik an der Selbstaufhebung einer wertneutralen Verfassung in 'Legalität und Legitimität.'" *Deutsche Vierteljahrsschrift für Literaturwissenschaft und Geistesgeschichte* 61 (1987): 1–34.

———. *Wahrheit und Geschichte: Studien zur Struktur der Philosophiegeschichte unter paradigmatischer Analyse der Entwicklung von Parmenides bis Platon.* Elea 1. Stuttgart–Bad Cannstatt: Frommann-Holzboog, 1984.

Hutchinson, George P. "The Nazi Ideology of Alfred Rosenberg: A Study of His Thought 1917–1946." D. Phil. dissertation, Oxford University, 1977.

Jens, Inge. *Dichter zwischen rechts und links: Die Geschichte der Sektion für Dichtkunst an der Preußischen Akademie der Künste dargestellt nach den Dokumenten.* Munich: Deutscher Taschenbuch Verlag, 1979.

Jermann, Christoph. *Philosophie und Politik: Untersuchungen zur Struktur und Problematik des Platonischen Idealismus.* Elea 2. Stuttgart–Bad Cannstatt: Frommann-Holzboog, 1986.

Jungrichter, Cornelia. *Ideologie und Tradition: Studien zur nationalsozialistischen Sonettdichtung.* Bonn: Bouvier, 1979.

Kaufmann, Walter. *Nietzsche: Philosopher, Psychologist, Antichrist.* 4th ed. Princeton: Princeton University Press, 1974.

Kerényi, Karl. "Zum Verhältnis von Vergilius Aeneis B. VI. (Randbemerkun-

gen zu Nordens Kommentar)." *Hermes: Zeitschrift für klassische Philologie* 66 (1931): 413–41.
Ketelsen, Uwe-K. "Nationalsozialismus und Drittes Reich." In *Geschichte der politischen Lyrik in Deutschland*, edited by Walter Hinderer, 291–314. Stuttgart: Reclam, 1978.
―――. "NS—Literatur und Modernität." In *Deutschsprachige Exilliteratur: Studien zu ihrer Bestimmung im Kontext der Epoche 1930 bis 1960*, edited by Wulf Koepke and Michael Winkler, 37–55. Studien zur Literatur der Moderne 12. Bonn: Bouvier, 1984.
Klemperer, Victor. *LTI: Notizbuch eines Philologen*. Berlin: Aufbau, 1947.
Klieneberger, H. R. *The Christian Writers of the Inner Emigration*. British Studies in Germanic Languages and Literatures. The Hague: Mouton, 1968.
Köhn, Lothar. "Überwindung des Historismus: Zu Problemen einer Geschichte der deutschen Literatur zwischen 1918 und 1933." *Deutsche Vierteljahrsschrift für Literaturwissenschaft und Geistesgeschichte* 47 (1974): 704–66; 49 (1975): 94–165.
Kolb, David. *The Critique of Pure Modernity: Hegel, Heidegger, and After*. Chicago: University of Chicago Press, 1986.
Krieger, Murray. "*Ekphrasis* and the Still Movement of Poetry; or, Laokoön Revisited." In *The Poet as Critic*, edited by Frederick P. W. McDowell, 3–26. Evanston: Northwestern University Press, 1967.
Krockow, Christian Graf von. *Die Entscheidung: Eine Untersuchung über Ernst Jünger, Carl Schmitt, Martin Heidegger*. Stuttgart: Enke, 1958.
Kuhlmann, Wolfgang. *Reflexive Letztbegründung: Untersuchungen zur Transzendentalpragmatik*. Freiburg: Alber, 1985.
Loewy, Ernst. *Literatur unterm Hakenkreuz: Das Dritte Reich und seine Dichtung. Eine Dokumentation*. Fischer Taschenbuch 4303. Frankfurt am Main: Fischer, 1966.
Lohner, Edgar. *Passion und Intellekt. Die Lyrik Gottfried Benns*. Neuwied: Luchterhand, 1961.
Löwenthal, Richard. "Widerstand im totalen Staat." In *Widerstand und Verweigerung in Deutschland 1933 bis 1945*, edited by Richard Löwenthal and Patrik von zu Mühlen, 11–24. Berlin: Dietz, 1982.
Magnus, Bernd. *Nietzsche's Existential Imperative*. Bloomington: Indiana University Press, 1978.
Malten, Ludolf. "Ein alexandrinisches Gedicht vom Raube der Kore." *Hermes: Zeitschrift für classische Philologie* 45 (1910): 506–53.
Manyoni, Angelika. *Consistency of Phenotype. A Study of Gottfried Benn's Views on Lyric Poetry*. Bern: Lang, 1983.
Margolis, Joseph. *Pragmatism without Foundations: Reconciling Realism and Relativism*. Oxford: Blackwell, 1986.
Maurach, Gregor. "Gottfried Benn und die Antike." *Acta Germanica* 5 (1970): 203–13.
Melin, Charlotte, and Cecile Cazort Zorach. "Cuba as Paradise, Paradigm, and Paradox in German Literature." *Monatshefte* 78 (1986): 480–99.

Meyer, Theo. *Kunstproblematik und Wortkombinatorik bei Gottfried Benn*. Kölner germanistische Studien 6. Cologne: Böhlau, 1971.
Nehamas, Alexander. *Nietzsche: Literature as Life*. Cambridge: Harvard University Press, 1985.
Nova, Fritz. *Alfred Rosenberg: Nazi Theorist of the Holocaust*. New York: Hippocrene, 1986.
Petzold, Joachim. "Zur Funktion des Nationalismus: Moeller van den Brucks Beitrag zur faschistischen Ideologie." *Zeitschrift für Geschichtswissenschaft* 11 (1973): 1285–1300.
Reichel, Peter. *Künstlermoral. Das Formalismus-Programm spätbürgerlicher Dichtung in Gottfried Benns 'gereimter Weltanschauung.'* Zur Kritik der bürgerlichen Ideologie 42. Frankfurt am Main: Verlag Marxistische Blätter, 1974.
———. "Die 'Statischen Gedichte' im Spätwerk Gottfried Benns." Diss. Leipzig, 1971.
Ritchie, J. M. *German Literature under National Socialism*. Totowa, N.J.: Barnes and Noble, 1983.
Roche, Mark W. *Dynamic Stillness: Philosophical Conceptions of Ruhe in Schiller, Hölderlin, Büchner, and Heine*. Studien zur deutschen Literatur 92. Tübingen: Niemeyer, 1987.
———. "Plato and the Structures of Injustice." In *Inquiries into Values: The Inaugural Session of the International Society for Value Inquiry*, edited by Sander H. Lee, 279–90. Problems in Contemporary Philosophy 11. Lewiston, N.Y.: Mellen, 1988.
Ryan, Judith. "Ezra Pound und Gottfried Benn: Avantgarde, Faschismus und ästhetische Autonomie." In *Faschismus und Avantgarde*, edited by Reinhold Grimm and Jost Hermand, 20–34. Königstein/Ts.: Athenäum, 1980.
Schnell, Ralf. "Innere Emigration und kulturelle Dissidenz." In *Widerstand und Verweigerung in Deutschland 1933 bis 1945*, edited by Richard Löwenthal and Patrik von zu Mühlen, 211–25. Berlin: Dietz, 1982.
———. *Literarische Innere Emigration 1933–1945*. Stuttgart: Metzler, 1976.
Scholl, Inge. *Die weiße Rose*. 2nd ed. Frankfurt: Verlag der Frankfurter Hefte, 1952.
Schonauer, Franz. *Deutsche Literatur im Dritten Reich. Versuch einer Darstellung in polemisch-didaktischer Absicht*. Olten: Walter-Verlag, 1961.
Schröder, Jürgen. *Gottfried Benn. Poesie und Sozialisation*. Stuttgart: Kohlhammer, 1978.
———. *Gottfried Benn und die Deutschen: Studien zu Werk, Person und Zeitgeschichte*. Stauffenberg Colloquium 1. Tübingen: Stauffenberg, 1986.
Schulte-Sasse, Jochen. *Literarische Wertung*. Stuttgart: Metzler, 1971.
Schulte-Sasse, Linda. "The Jew as Other under National Socialism: Veit Harlan's 'Jud Süss.' " *German Quarterly* 61 (1988): 22–49.
Schwerte, Hans. *Faust und das Faustische: Ein Kapitel deutscher Ideologie*. Stuttgart: Klett, 1962.
Seidler, Ingo. "Statische Montage. Zur poetischen Technik im Spätwerk Gottfried Benns." *Monatshefte* 52 (1960): 321–30.

Smith, Barbara Herrnstein. *Contingencies of Value: Alternative Perspectives for Critical Theory.* Cambridge: Harvard University Press, 1988.

Steinhagen, Harald. "Gottfried Benn 1933." In *Literatur und Germanistik nach der 'Machtübernahme.' Colloquium zur 50. Wiederkehr des 30. Januar 1933,* edited by Beda Allemann, 28–51. Bonn: Bouvier, 1983.

———. *Die Statischen Gedichte von Gottfried Benn. Die Vollendung seiner expressionistischen Lyrik.* Stuttgart: Klett, 1969.

Stern, Fritz. "National Socialism as Temptation." In his *Dreams and Delusions: The Drama of German History,* 147–91. New York: Knopf, 1987.

———. *The Politics of Cultural Despair.* Berkeley: University of California Press, 1961.

Stern, J. P. "Adalbert Stifter: '*Erhebung* without Motion.' " In his *Idylls and Realities: Studies in Nineteenth-Century German Literature,* 97–122. London: Methuen, 1971.

Stollmann, Rainer. *Ästhetisierung der Politik: Literaturstudien zum subjektiven Faschismus.* Stuttgart: Metzler, 1978.

———. "Gottfried Benn. Zum Verhältnis von Ästhetizismus und Faschismus." *Text und Kontext* 8 (1980): 284–308.

Vahland, Joachim. "Sind die 'Statischen Gedichte' statische Gedichte?" In *Gottfried Benn,* edited by Bruno Hillebrand, 350–66. Wege der Forschung 316. Darmstadt: Wissenschaftliche Buchgesellschaft, 1979.

Vitzthum, Wolfgang Graf. "Brochs demokratie- und völkerbundtheoretische Schriften." In *Hermann Broch,* edited by Paul Michael Lützeler, 289–307. Suhrkamp Taschenbuch 2065. Frankfurt am Main: Suhrkamp, 1986.

Wandschneider, Dieter. "Die Absolutheit des Logischen und das Sein der Natur. Systematische Überlegungen zum absolut-idealistischen Ansatz Hegels." *Zeitschrift für philosophische Forschung* 39 (1985): 331–51.

———. "Die dialektische Notwendigkeit des Negativen und ihre ethische Relevanz." *Hegel-Jahrbuch* (1987): 185–94.

Weber, Regina. *Gottfried Benn. Zwischen Christentum und Gnosis.* Bern: Lang, 1983.

Wellershoff, Dieter. *Gottfried Benn: Phänotyp dieser Stunde: Eine Studie über den Problemgehalt seines Werkes.* Cologne: Kiepenheuer, 1958.

Whisker, James Biser. *The Social, Political and Religious Thought of Alfred Rosenberg: An Interpretive Essay.* Washington, D.C.: University Press of America, 1982.

Willems, Gottfried. *Großstadt- und Bewußtseinspoesie: Über den Realismus in der modernen Lyrik, insbesondere im lyrischen Spätwerk Gottfried Benns und in der deutschen Lyrik seit 1965.* Untersuchungen zur deutschen Literaturgeschichte 31. Tübingen: Niemeyer, 1981.

Winternitz, Moriz. *Geschichte der indischen Litteratur.* 3 vols. Leipzig: Amelangs, 1920.

Wodtke, Friedrich Wilhelm. "Die Antike im Werk Gottfried Benns." *Orbis Litterarum* 16 (1961): 129–238.

———. *Gottfried Benn*. 2nd ed. Stuttgart: Metzler, 1970.

Ziolkowski, Theodore. "Form als Protest: Das Sonett in der Literatur des Exils und der Inneren Emigration." In *Exil und innere Emigration*, edited by Reinhold Grimm and Jost Hermand, 153–72. Third Wisconsin Workshop. Frankfurt am Main: Athenäum, 1972.

Index

Absolute, 11–12, 22, 79; absolute poetry, 21
Action, activism, 24–25, 48
Aestheticism, 70
Aesthetic method, 4, 75
Aesthetic worth, 76–77
Alter, Reinhard, 39
Ambiguity, 76–77
Angelus Silesius, 31
Apollo, Apollinian, 6, 10–11, 13–15, 27, 38, 46, 86 (n. 25)
Aristotle, 37
Art: therapeutic function of, 10, 54–55; art and politics, 39–42, 65–70; art and philosophy, 70, 72
Asian, anti-Asian, 25, 46–48, 88 (n. 16)

Baroque, 86 (n. 4), 91 (n. 15)
Benn, Gottfried: "Trunkene Flut," 2, 5–15, 17–19, 28, 37, 45, 70, 72, 75, 77, 80; "Wer allein ist—," 2, 15–22, 24–25, 44–45, 67, 70, 72, 75, 80; "Statische Gedichte," 2, 23–29, 33, 37–38, 44–45, 49, 54, 68–71, 73, 75, 77, 80; "Reisen," 2, 30–38, 45, 54, 66, 72, 75, 77, 80
Bewegung, 25, 44–50
Biology, biological, 16–17, 24, 40, 61
Blue, 7, 13
Böhm, Franz, 97 (n. 39)
Bonaventure, Saint, 32
Brecht, Bertolt, 89 (n. 6)
Broch, Hermann, 56, 62

Children, 24
Christ, 8
Christianity, 53
Circles, circularity, 11–12, 28–29, 36–37, 50
Classicism, *Klassik*, 21–22, 48
Closure, 11–13, 21, 29, 35, 46, 105 (n. 29)
Contradiction, 41, 56–61, 63, 71, 77–79, 106 (n. 4)
Creation, 6, 8, 10, 13, 17, 37, 40

Dada, 32–33
Death, 27; revival of the dead, 8–10
Decisionism, 41, 58, 66–67, 70, 78
Demeter, 7–11, 84 (n. 4)
Desert, 30–31, 33–34
Diettrich, Fritz, 51
Dionysus, Dionysian, 6–11, 13–14
Disorientation, 51, 66–67, 81
Droste-Hülshoff, Annette von, 9–10
Dynamic, Dynamism, 10, 45–48, 83 (n. 1)

Eckhart, Meister, 31, 47, 90 (n. 4), 96 (n. 32)
Eichendorff, Joseph von, 35
Emptiness, 34
Ethics, 71
Etymology, etymological, 35–36
Evola, Julius, 48
Exotic, 30–34, 91 (n. 7)
Experience, 35–36, 43, 66

Fatalism, 25, 72
Faustian, anti-Faustian, 2, 21, 38, 44–47
Fichte, Johann Gottlieb, 25
Flux, 6, 15, 17, 20, 52, 87 (n. 16)
Form, Formalism, 21, 40, 42, 65–70, 78–79
Foxglove, 10, 12–13
Friedrich, Hugo, 1

Genetic fallacy, 75–76
Geology, geological, 16–17
God, 31–32, 37
Goethe, Johann Wolfgang von, 21; concept of *die Mütter*, 9, 18, 85 (n. 15); "Selige Sehnsucht," 18; "Prometheus," 36–37; "Natur und Kunst," 87 (n. 14). *See also* Faustian
Greek, anti-Greek, 46–48, 88 (n. 16)

Hagelstange, Rudolf, 51–52, 68
Havana, 31–32
Hegel, G. W. F., 4, 17, 19, 21, 27, 60, 69, 88 (n. 4), 105 (n. 28)
Heidegger, Martin, 66–67

Heine, Heinrich, 21
Heraclitus, Heraclitean, 16, 20, 44, 67
Hermes, 84 (n. 4)
History, 7–8, 17, 25–26, 42, 61, 73, 79
Hitler, Adolf, 40, 65, 67, 96 (n. 27), 97 (n. 39), 101 (n. 26)
Hoffmann, Charles, 54
Hölderlin, Friedrich, 13, 19
Humanity, 60–61

Ideologiekritik, 78
Immanent Critique, 63, 77–78
Indifference, 21, 69, 71–74, 88 (n. 1)
Ineffable, 16, 20
Injustice, 55, 58–59, 81
Inner emigration, 39, 43–55, 68, 73, 80
Inspiration, 28
Intellect, antiintellectualism, 24, 48
Intellectual history, intellectual-historical method, 3–4, 75–76

Jewish, anti-Semitic, 46–47
Jung, Carl, 7, 32
Jünger, Friedrich Georg, 51
Jungrichter, Cornelia, 68

Kant, Immanuel, 47
Kaufmann, Walter, 56
Ketelsen, Uwe-K., 67–68

Lao-tzu, 47, 88 (n. 5), 97 (n. 36)
Legal positivism, 62
Leip, Hans, 51
Lévy-Bruhl, Lucien, 84 (n. 3)
Limit, 21, 35–36, 38, 45
Logic, 4, 57, 60
Löwenthal, Richard, 42
Luther, Martin, 73

Mann, Thomas, 43, 103 (n. 2)
Meyer, Semi, 87–88 (n. 16)
Moeller van den Bruck, Arthur, 39, 66, 101–2 (n. 29)
Montage technique, 8
Mörike, Eduard, 15
Motion, movement, 17–18, 28, 33–34, 37, 50, 87 (n. 16)
Mysticism, mystical, 6, 16, 31–32, 72

National socialism, 24–25, 39–42, 56–68 passim, 81; national socialist poetry, 44, 48–49; national socialist film, 49–50
Nature, 58, 61
Nehamas, Alexander, 100 (n. 18)
Nemerov, Howard, 11
Nietzsche, Friedrich, 16, 24, 33, 41, 61, 63, 84 (n. 2), 86 (n. 25); and perspectivism, 27–28, 31, 57–59, 68–69; "Vereinsamt," 29, 31; concept of passive and active nihilism, 58, 69. *See also* Apollinian, Dionysian
Nihilism, 69–70
Nonemigration, 54
Norms, 43, 56, 60, 63, 78–79, 98 (n. 60), 99–100 (n. 13)
Novalis, 19

Odysseus, 8–10
Opitz, Martin, 90 (n. 2)
Ovid, 84 (n. 4)

Parmenides, 21
Perfection, 19–20
Persephone, 7, 84 (n. 4)
Perspective, 28, 68–69
Plato, 16, 21, 27, 58, 93 (n. 31)
Plessner, Helmuth, 102 (n. 33)
Power, power positivism, 41, 51, 57–59, 62, 69, 77
Prometheus, 8, 36–37, 85 (n. 9), 90 (n. 2), 93 (n. 29)
Protagoras, 16

Race, 58, 60–62
Reason, 52, 58, 61–62, 101 (n. 26)
Relativism, 25, 28, 57–63, 99 (n. 10)
Resistance, 73, 103 (n. 42); types of, 42–43
Rhyme, 11–12, 20
Riefenstahl, Leni: *Triumph des Willens*, 50, 66–67
Rilke, Rainer Maria, 18, 83 (n. 1)
Rimbaud, 85 (n. 14)
Romanticism, 21, 35
Rosenberg, Alfred: critique of *Statik*, 46–48, 52; critique of absolute truth and of logic, 52, 56, 59–62

Sacrifice, 7, 10, 12, 19, 24, 44
Sage, 23–29
Schirach, Baldur von, 50
Schmitt, Carl, 62
Schopenhauer, Arthur, 89 (n. 16), 92 (n. 28)
Sculpture, 11, 21–22, 46, 49
Seasons, 7, 11
Secondary virtues, 24, 44, 58, 103 (n. 6)
Self-cancellation, figure of, 58–59, 63, 71, 77–78, 90 (n. 20), 99 (n. 9), 102 (n. 38)
Seneca, 34–36, 72, 91 (n. 15)
Sexuality, 6–7, 10, 17
Shadow, 16, 26–27
Shaftesbury, Anthony, Earl of, 37
Silence, 20, 79, 90 (n. 20)
Smith, Barbara Herrnstein, 100 (n. 16)
Socrates, 60
Sonnet, 68
Spengler, Oswald, 38, 46, 94 (n. 35)
Statik, 2–3, 44–48, 50, 52, 72–74, 83 (n. 5)
Steinhoff, Hans: *Hitlerjunge Quex*, 49–50
Stifter, Adalbert, 36, 92 (nn. 22, 24)
Stillness: varieties of, 3, 26, 36–37, 80
Stoicism, Stoics, 23, 25, 34, 72, 88 (n. 4)
Subjectivity, subjectivism, 17, 70–71
Suffering, 8, 10, 85 (n. 10)

Thieß, Frank, 43
Time, temporality, 17–18, 20, 49
Timelessness, 8, 21, 26, 43, 49, 52, 54–55, 68
Totality, 42, 65, 73, 105 (n. 37)
Transcendence, 52, 54–55, 62–66, 73, 81
Travel, 24, 26, 30, 32, 34–36, 54

Unconscious, 7, 9
Unmoved mover, 37

Values, 24; universal values, 43, 52–53, 60, 74; partial value systems, 56, 62–63

Water, 7, 11, 17, 20
Weber, Regina, 71
Weimar Constitution, 62
Wholeness, 20, 28
Wiechert, Ernst, 52–54
Will, 25, 41, 67
Winckelmann, Johann Joachim, 3, 21
Withdrawal, 25, 36, 48, 53, 73, 79, 88 (n. 4)

Youth, 49

Ziolkowski, Theodore, 68
Zurich, 31–33

www.ingramcontent.com/pod-product-compliance
Lightning Source LLC
Chambersburg PA
CBHW031316150426
43191CB00005B/260